THE TWO GENTLEMEN OF VERONA

The RSC Shakespeare

Edited by Jonathan Bate and Eric Rasmussen

Chief Associate Editors: Jan Sewell and Will Sharpe

Associate Editors: Trey Jansen, Eleanor Lowe, Lucy Munro,
Dee Anna Phares, Héloïse Sénéchal

The Two Gentlemen of Verona

Textual editing: Eric Rasmussen

Introduction and Shakespeare's Career in the Theater: Jonathan Bate

Commentary: Héloïse Sénéchal

Scene-by-Scene Analysis: Jan Sewell

In Performance: Jan Sewell (RSC stagings) and Peter Kirwan (overview)

The Director's Cut (interviews by Jan Sewell and Kevin Wright):
David Thacker and Edward Hall

Editorial Advisory Board

Gregory Doran, Chief Associate Director, Royal Shakespeare Company

Jim Davis, Professor of Theatre Studies, University of Warwick, UK

Charles Edelman, Senior Lecturer, Edith Cowan University,
Western Australia

Lukas Erne, Professor of Modern English Literature,
Université de Genève, Switzerland

Jacqui O'Hanlon, Director of Education, Royal Shakespeare Company

Akiko Kusunoki, Tokyo Woman's Christian University, Japan

Ron Rosenbaum, author and journalist, New York, USA

James Shapiro, Professor of English and Comparative Literature,
Columbia University, USA

Tiffany Stern, Professor and Tutor in English, University of Oxford, UK

The RSC Shakespeare

William Shakespeare

THE TWO GENTLEMEN OF VERONA

Edited by Jonathan Bate and Eric Rasmussen

Introduced by Jonathan Bate

The Modern Library
New York

CONTENTS

INTRODUCTION

ORIGINS

The Two Gentlemen of Verona is one of Shakespeare's early plays, perhaps even his first. We do not know exactly when it was written or
first performed, but its stylistic and dramatic features mark it out as
early work: a small cast, a preponderance of end-stopped verse lines,
a degree of simplicity in both language and characterization.
Though the play has the relative superficiality of youth, it also has
the virtues of that time of life: freshness, energy, pace, wholeheart-
edness, a desire to get to the point and to speak its mind. It is about
the things that matter most urgently to young people: themselves,
their friendships and their love affairs. It makes its drama out of the
conflicts between these things: how can you be simultaneously true
to yourself, to your best friend, and to the object of your sexual
desire? Especially if the person you've fallen in love with happens to
be your best friend's girlfriend.

Shakespeare and his contemporaries inherited their idea of
stage comedy from the ancient Roman masters Terence and Plau-
tus. According to the classical model, whereas tragedy concerned
itself with heroes and kings, with wars and affairs of state, comedy
was about ordinary people—people like us. Elizabethan audiences
expected to be stirred to amazement by the matter of tragedy, but to
see images of themselves in a comedy.

Classical comedy wove a set of variations on a common theme.
Boy meets girl. Girl's father is not amused: he has another suitor in
mind, a richer, older, or better-connected man. But, often thanks to
the assistance of an ingenious servant, the young lovers overcome
all obstacles and are united. Confusion, disguises, and mistaken
identity abound along the way. Stories of this kind recur throughout
European Renaissance culture, in both prose romance and stage
comedy. Thus in *The Two Gentlemen* the Duke intends to marry his

daughter Silvia to the foolish Turio, so Valentine arrives with a letter, a rope ladder, and the intention to elope with her by night. The Shakespearean twist in the tale is that the person who has tipped off the Duke about Valentine's intentions is the latter's best friend Proteus, who has also fallen in love with Silvia.

One of the plays in the repertoire of the Queen's Men, the leading acting company of the 1580s, was recorded under the title *The History of Felix and Feliomena* (probably a transcription error for *Felismena*). It was a dramatization of a story in the Portuguese writer Jorge de Montemayor's *Diana*, a multiply plotted prose romance of the 1540s that was read and imitated across Europe. A French translation was published in the 1570s and an English one undertaken in the 1580s, though not published until 1598. The Queen's Men play is lost, but it presumably followed the basic outline of Montemayor's plot. On seeing the beautiful Celia, Don Felix deserts his lover Felismena. The latter disguises herself as a page boy and follows him. Celia then falls in love with the page. She is rejected and dies. Felismena's identity is revealed and she is reunited with Don Felix.

Shakespeare clearly knew this story. He is unlikely to have had enough Spanish or even French to have read it in published form, so his knowledge was probably based on a script or a viewing of the Queen's Men play, or even on having acted in it himself. It is just possible that he saw the manuscript of the English version of Montemayor—perhaps whoever wrote the play for the Queen's Men possessed a copy of the Don Felix section.

The mark of Shakespeare's originality was his gift of combining disparate sources. He created *The Two Gentlemen of Verona* by turning Felix, Felismena, and Celia into Proteus, Julia, and Silvia while simultaneously mapping this love triangle onto another one, namely the plot of two friends falling out with each other by falling in love with the same girl.

One of the most influential prose romances—one might say protonovels—in Elizabethan England was John Lyly's *Euphues*, published in 1578. It told the story of two close male friends who fall in love with the same girl. The narrative serves as the field for a debate about the conflicting demands of friendship and erotic desire. At the same time, Lyly established a dichotomy between two kinds of education, the intellectual (symbolized by Athens, ancient Greece being the seat of wisdom) and the sentimental (symbolized by Naples, Italy being the playground of lovers). One character stays home in Athens, while the other travels to Naples.

The story line of *Euphues* had innumerable precedents, going back through the Middle Ages to ancient times. Some were tragic, some comic. A famous example was the tale of bosom friends and fellow warriors Palamon and Arcite. Chaucer's *Knight's Tale* tells of how they both fall for a lady named Emilia, with tragic consequences. At the very end of his career, Shakespeare would dramatize their story in a play cowritten with John Fletcher: *The Two Noble Kinsmen*. As the similarity in title suggests, this is a revisiting of *The Two Gentlemen* in a different key, testimony to the endurance of Shakespeare's interest in the motif of male bonding versus heterosexual desire—which he also explored in works as diverse as *Othello*, *The Winter's Tale*, and the *Sonnets*.

DEBATES

In all sorts of ways, *The Two Gentlemen* is a prototype for later Shakespearean developments. The cross-dressed heroine recurs in the more renowned comedies of the late 1590s and early 1600s. The outlaw scenes introduce a movement out from "civil" society into a "wilderness" or green world, where surprising developments take place, anticipating the enchanted wood of *A Midsummer Night's Dream* and the Forest of Arden in *As You Like It*. The soliloquies of Proteus, meanwhile, offer an early example of a Shakespearean character undergoing a crisis of personal identity, of consciousness—already we are moving into the territory that will be taken in very different (and of course much more complex) directions in the self-communion of Richard III, Richard II, and eventually Hamlet.

The play begins by establishing the friendship between the two gentlemen. Valentine's name suggests the patron saint of lovers in the Christian tradition, while that of Proteus evokes the shape-changing god of the classical tradition. The names are enough to suggest that Valentine will be the constant lover, Proteus the fickle one. Initially, though, Valentine is associated with the pursuit of "honour" rather than sexual desire. He intends to seek his fortune in the city of Milan instead of "living dully sluggardized at home." His plan would immediately have pricked the interest of many members of the play's original London audience, who would themselves have made the journey from the provinces to the capital—as indeed Shakespeare had done himself not long before writing the play.

Proteus, meanwhile, has undergone a psychological rather than a physical journey: he has left himself, his friends, and all, for love. His desire for Julia has "metamorphosed" him and made him neglect his studies, waste his time, and go to "War with good counsel." The didactic literature of the age was full of admonitions against such self-abuse. Young gentlemen were supposed to study the arts of good behavior and good citizenship, not to be distracted by affairs of the heart and effeminizing influences. Stage plays came into the latter category, which partially accounts for the anti-theatrical diatribes of Elizabethan "puritans."

The notion of drama as debate, developed in large measure from the plays of Lyly, led Shakespeare to write his opening scenes as a series of two-handers. First we have Valentine and Proteus, debating the relative merits of erotic desire and civic honor. Then Julia and her knowing maid Lucetta debate how a girl should respond to a proposition of love. And then the representatives of the older generation, Proteus' father, Antonio, and the servant Pantino, discuss the need for a young man to be tested in the world before he can achieve maturity.

As well as establishing oppositions between generations and genders, Shakespeare also sets up a dialogue across the barrier of class by means of witty banter between master and servant. Valentine goes to Milan in pursuit of honor, but once he gets there he finds himself in the same situation as Proteus back in Verona: "metamorphosed with a mistress." His mockery of lovers' affectation in the first scene comes back to haunt him. Meanwhile his servant Speed is there to anatomize the characteristics of the mooning courtly lover: he observes his master folding his arms like a melancholy malcontent, relishing love songs, walking alone, sighing like a schoolboy who knows he's going to be in trouble for losing his spelling book, weeping, speaking in a whining voice, and rejecting food like someone on a diet. Much as the play celebrates the transforming energies

of young love—and indeed engages with its destructive potential—
it also mocks the courtly idiom of love language, not least through
the contrast between the artificial poeticisms of the genteel characters and the robust prose voice of their servants.

The name "Speed" suggests the quickness of wit that is confirmed
by this servant's linguistic facility and awareness of the gentlemen's
foibles. He always seems to be one step ahead of Valentine, anticipating what his master's going to do next in an aside shared with the
audience. Proteus' servant Lance also has a name that suggests
mental sharpness: Shakespeare himself was often praised by his contemporaries for having a wit that was as sharp as the spear in his
name. Ironically, though, Lance's way of proceeding is anything but
pointed: his role is that of the clown for whom everything goes
wrong and who confuses his words ("the prodigious son" for "the
prodigal son," "a notable lover" misheard as "A notable lubber").
When he tries to use his shoe, his staff, his hat, and his dog to act out
the scene of his farewell from his family, he gets into a terrible tangle.
The joke is that this should be as a result of the unpredictability of
the live dog onstage, but actually it is due to Lance's own incompe-
tence. At the end of the fourth act, Lance has a second two-hander
with his dog, Crab, a riff on the theme of a servant's obedience to his
master. As Lance makes a mess of the demands of Proteus, so Crab
fails to do the will of Lance: "did not I bid thee still mark me and do
as I do? When didst thou see me heave up my leg and make water
against a gentlewoman's farthingale?"

While Speed mocks Valentine's transformation into a lover, Lance
succumbs to desire in the manner of his master. He falls in love with
a milkmaid, the unseen prototype of the hoyden character type that
will be incarnated in the fat kitchen maid of *The Comedy of Errors*
and *As You Like It*'s goatherd Audrey. Lance's catalogue of the milkmaid's down-to-earth virtues and vices parodies the courtly lover's
enumeration of the beauties of his mistress.

LOVERS

In the world of Shakespearean comedy, young women are usually
seen in one of three settings. With their parents, where they are

expected to be obedient, which ultimately means marrying the man of the parents' choice. With a female confidante, such as a servant or kinswoman, in whose company they can talk of love. And in a position of vulnerability, away from home, where their courage is tested and they have to live by their wits (for example, by taking on male disguise), but where they have unprecedented freedom to explore and express their true selves, their hopes, fears, and desires. Silvia enters in the first role, under the eye of her father, the Duke of Milan, as he measures up her potential suitors. The beautiful lady of courtly romance, she is the object of men's devoted gaze and fantastic desire, a woman on a pedestal who reveals little of her inner life. Julia, by contrast, wears her heart upon her sleeve as she moves from the second to the third of the female situations when she sets off in pursuit of Proteus. Her decision to do so reveals the sexual double standard that was pervasive in Shakespeare's time: whereas a young man is condemned for "sluggardizing" at home, a young woman risks being made the object of scandal by setting out from home.

One of Shakespeare's favorite techniques was the dramatically ironic counterpointing of scenes: we see Julia proving her love for Proteus by setting off on her dangerous journey immediately after we have seen Proteus renouncing his love for Julia because he has been smitten by the sight of Silvia. The scene when Valentine introduces his best friend to the girl he has fallen in love with is brief but very subtly written. It turns on the correspondence between the language of courtesy and that of courtship. Valentine asks Silvia to welcome Proteus "with some special favour" and to "entertain him" in her service. What he means is "please treat my friend with respect," but since in the courtly idiom the language of service is synonymous with that of love, Proteus is given an opening to project himself into the role of a rival lover—when Silvia modestly refers to herself as a "worthless mistress" he responds by saying that he would fight to the death anyone else who described her thus. In a sense, the crux of the play lies in the double meaning of the word "mistress."

Proteus explores his own transformation in two soliloquies that come in rapid succession. In the first, he introduces the image of his love for Julia as akin to a wax image melted to oblivion by the heat of his new desire for Silvia. At the same time, he recognizes that what he has fallen in love with is merely a "picture," the outer image of her beauty. The play begins to probe more deeply into the nature of love when in later scenes a series of questions are asked about the relationship between the "shadow" of surface beauty and the "substance" or "essence" of personality within. In parallel with this motif, the action develops the concerns of Proteus' second major soliloquy: making and breaking vows, finding and losing selves, and the conflict between "sweet-suggesting Love" and "the law of friendship." "In love," Proteus asks at the play's crisis point, "Who respects friend?"

Prior to the last few years of Shakespeare's career, his plays were performed without interval. Despite this, there is often a perceptible change in the action at the beginning of the fourth act. The plot has been wound to the full, so now the unwinding begins. Here the turning point is marked by the movement away from court and city to a wood peopled by some rather genteel Outlaws. One of them swears "By the bare scalp of Robin Hood's fat friar," and it is the jolly camaraderie of the merry men, stripped of the old story's violence and political edge, that is evoked by these Outlaws.

Desire feeds itself on rejection. The more Silvia spurns Proteus, the more he desires her. By the same account, the more he spurns Julia, the more she dotes on him. In the play's richest sequence, music is introduced to establish a nocturnal setting in which Proteus displaces Turio and woos Silvia at her window, not knowing that he is overheard by Julia in her page-boy disguise: This is her dark night of the soul. But then in a bold and very Shakespearean twist, when Proteus confronts the disguised Julia face-to-face he takes rather a fancy to her boy self: "Sebastian is thy name? I like thee well and will employ thee in some service presently." The words "employ" and "service" maintain the punning on the shared language of domestic obligation and sexual engagement. Anticipating Viola in *Twelfth Night*, Julia finds herself in the painful position of being "servant" to the man whose "mistress" she really wants to be. Hitherto Proteus has regarded Julia as nothing more than a decorative blonde. Now that he thinks she is Sebastian, he unwittingly begins to intuit her inner qualities.

At this point, the play reaches its highest point of sophistication and self-conscious artfulness. The audience is offered two images: a portrait of Silvia and a description of Sebastian, dressed in Julia's clothes, playing the part of a rejected lover, Ariadne deserted by Theseus in a famous story from classical mythology. The contrast between the two images effectively turns the scene into a Shakespearean claim for the superiority not only of the player's art to the portrait painter's but also of his own dramatization of love to the static vision of courtly romance. The painting, like the lady of romance, is but a "senseless form" to be "worshipped, kissed, loved and adored." The actor, by contrast, can evoke the real pain of passion so convincingly ("so lively acted") that the audience may be moved to tears. No one is better than Proteus at expressing eternal adoration in the artful language—all sighs and poetic hyperbole—of the courtly lover, but his fickleness reveals the essential insincerity of the code. Paradoxically, it is the play actor who is truly sincere: "Sebastian" is really Julia, passioning not for Theseus' but for Proteus' perjury and unjust flight.

Painters can achieve tricks of the eye—perspectival illusions of depth, anamorphic representations that vary in appearance according to where the viewer stands—but the theatrical imagination can do much more: the imagined performance of Sebastian as Ariadne is mapped onto the achieved performance of both Julia as Sebastian in the world of the play and the boy actor as Julia on the stage where the drama was first brought to life. Throughout his career, Shakespeare will return to such complex layered effects of illusion and reality, in accordance with his core belief that we are all players in the great theater of the world.

Having gone emotionally deep in the fourth act, Shakespeare speeds toward a conventional comic conclusion in the fifth. The forest of the jolly Outlaws is his device for doing so. It is not a psychologically complex environment, like the wood in *A Midsummer Night's Dream*. Rather, it is a place where the polished veneer of civil society is stripped away, allowing people to act impulsively on their desires. Proteus wants Silvia, so he threatens to rape her. Proteus asks forgiveness, so Valentine seeks to demonstrate that he values friendship above love by offering him Silvia. Sebastian reveals that s/he is Julia, so Proteus recognizes that he really loved her all along. Turio comes on to claim Silvia but instantly recognizes that only a fool "will endanger / His body for a girl that loves him not." The father is won round and the play is over. This is the ending we expect and desire, but the abruptness with which it comes about is a sign of impatience or immaturity on Shakespeare's part—but then again, his mind was so restlessly inventive that he never really cared for endings.

ABOUT THE TEXT

Shakespeare endures through history. He illuminates later times as well as his own. He helps us to understand the human condition. But he cannot do this without a good text of the plays. Without editions there would be no Shakespeare. That is why every twenty years or so throughout the last three centuries there has been a major new edition of his complete works. One aspect of editing is the process of keeping the texts up to date—modernizing the spelling, punctuation, and typography (though not, of course, the actual words), providing explanatory notes in the light of changing educational practices (a generation ago, most of Shakespeare's classical and biblical allusions could be assumed to be generally understood, but now they can't).

Because Shakespeare did not personally oversee the publication of his plays, with some plays there are major editorial difficulties. Decisions have to be made as to the relative authority of the early printed editions, the pocket format "Quartos" published in Shakespeare's lifetime and the elaborately produced "First Folio" text of 1623, the original "Complete Works" prepared for the press after his death by Shakespeare's fellow actors, the people who knew the plays better than anyone else. *The Two Gentlemen of Verona*, however, exists only in a Folio text that is generally well printed so there is little textual debate about this play.

The following notes highlight various aspects of the editorial process and indicate conventions used in the text of this edition:

Lists of Parts are supplied in the First Folio for only six plays, one of which is *The Two Gentlemen of Verona*, so the list here is based on "Names of all the Actors" at the end of the play. Capitals indicate that part of the name used for speech headings in the script (thus "SPEED, a clownish servant to Valentine").

Locations are provided by Folio for only two plays, of which *The Two Gentlemen of Verona* is not one. Eighteenth-century editors, working in an age of elaborately realistic stage sets, were the first to provide detailed locations (*"another part of the forest"*). Given that Shakespeare wrote for a bare stage and often an imprecise sense of place, we have relegated locations to the explanatory notes at the foot of the page, where they are given at the beginning of each scene where the imaginary location is different from the one before. In the case of *The Two Gentlemen of Verona*, the action moves between the Italian cities of Verona and Milan and the countryside round about.

Act and Scene Divisions were provided in Folio in a much more thoroughgoing way than in the Quartos. Sometimes, however, they were erroneous or omitted; corrections and additions supplied by editorial tradition are indicated by square brackets. Five-act division is based on a classical model, and act breaks provided the opportunity to replace the candles in the indoor Blackfriars playhouse, which the King's Men used after 1608, but Shakespeare did not necessarily think in terms of a five-part structure of dramatic composition. The Folio convention is that a scene ends when the stage is empty. Nowadays, partly under the influence of film, we tend to consider a scene to be a dramatic unit that ends with either a change of imaginary location or a significant passage of time within the narrative. Shakespeare's fluidity of composition accords well with this convention, so in addition to act and scene numbers we provide a *running scene* count in the right margin at the beginning of each new scene, in the typeface used for editorial directions. Where there is a scene break caused by a momentary bare stage, but the location does not change and extra time does not pass, we use the convention *running scene continues*. There is inevitably a degree of editorial judgment in making such calls, but the system is very valuable in suggesting the pace of the plays.

Speakers' Names are often inconsistent in Folio. We have regularized speech headings, but retained an element of deliberate inconsistency in entry directions, in order to give the flavor of Folio.

Verse is indicated by lines that do not run to the right margin and by capitalization of each line. The Folio printers sometimes set verse as prose, and vice versa (either out of misunderstanding or for reasons of space). We have silently corrected in such cases, although in some instances there is ambiguity, in which case we have leaned toward the preservation of Folio layout. Folio sometimes uses contraction ("turnd" rather than "turned") to indicate whether or not the final "-ed" of a past participle is sounded, an area where there is variation for the sake of the five-beat iambic pentameter rhythm. We use the convention of a grave accent to indicate sounding (thus "turnèd" would be two syllables), but would urge actors not to overstress. In cases where one speaker ends with a verse half-line and the next begins with the other half of the pentameter, editors since the late eighteenth century have indented the second line. We have abandoned this convention, since Folio does not use it, nor did actors' cues in the Shakespearean theater. An exception is made when the second speaker actively interrupts or completes the first speaker's sentence.

Spelling is modernized, but older forms are very occasionally maintained where necessary for rhythm or aural effect.

Punctuation in Shakespeare's time was as much rhetorical as grammatical. "Colon" was originally a term for a unit of thought in an argument. The semicolon was a new unit of punctuation (some of the Quartos lack them altogether). We have modernized punctuation throughout, but have given more weight to Folio punctuation than many editors, since, though not Shakespearean, it reflects the usage of his period. In particular, we have used the colon far more than many editors: it is exceptionally useful as a way of indicating how many Shakespearean speeches unfold clause by clause in a developing argument that gives the illusion of enacting the process of thinking in the moment. We have also kept in mind the origin of punctuation in classical times as a way of assisting the actor and orator: the comma suggests the briefest of pauses for breath, the colon a middling one, and a full stop or period a longer pause. Semicolons, by contrast, belong to an era of punctuation that was only just coming in during Shakespeare's time and that is coming to an end now: we have accordingly only used them where they occur in our copy texts (and not always then). Dashes are sometimes used for parenthetical interjections where the Folio has brackets. They are also used for interruptions and changes in train of thought. Where a change of addressee occurs within a speech, we have used a dash preceded by a period (or occasionally another form of punctuation). Often the identity of the respective addressees is obvious from the context. When it is not, this has been indicated in a marginal stage direction.

Entrances and Exits are fairly thorough in Folio, which has accordingly been followed as faithfully as possible. Where characters are omitted or corrections are necessary, this is indicated by square brackets (e.g. "[*and Attendants*]"). *Exit* is sometimes silently normalized to *Exeunt* and *Manet* anglicized to "remains." We trust Folio positioning of entrances and exits to a greater degree than most editors.

Editorial Stage Directions such as stage business, asides, indications of addressee and of characters' position on the gallery stage are only used sparingly in Folio. Other editions mingle directions of this kind with original Folio and Quarto directions, sometimes marking them by means of square brackets. We have sought to distinguish what could be described as *directorial* interventions of this kind from Folio-style directions (either original or supplied) by placing them in the right margin in a different typeface. There is a degree of subjectivity about which directions are of which kind, but the procedure is intended as a reminder to the reader and the actor that Shakespearean stage directions are often dependent upon editorial inference alone and are not set in stone. We also depart from editorial tradition in sometimes admitting uncertainty and thus printing permissive stage directions, such as an **Aside?** (often a line may be equally effective as an aside or a direct address—it is for each production or reading to make its own decision) or a **may exit** or a piece of business placed between arrows to indicate that it may occur at various moments within a scene.

Line Numbers in the left margin are editorial, for reference and to key the explanatory and textual notes.

Explanatory Notes at the foot of each page explain allusions and gloss obsolete and difficult words, confusing phraseology, occasional major textual cruces, and so on. Particular attention is given to non-standard usage, bawdy innuendo, and technical terms (e.g. legal and military language). Where more than one sense is given, commas indicate shades of related meaning, slashes alternative or double meanings.

Textual Notes at the end of the play indicate major departures from Folio. They take the following form: the reading of our text is given in bold and its source given after an equals sign with "Q" indicating a reading from the First Quarto of 1602, "Q3" a correction introduced in the Third Quarto of 1630, "F2" a correction that derives from the Second Folio of 1632, and "Ed" one that derives from the subsequent editorial tradition. The rejected Folio ("F") reading is then given. Thus for Act 4 Scene 2 line 114: "**4.2.114 his** = F2. F = her" means that we have adopted the correction of the Second Folio, when Silvia is discussing being buried in Valentine's grave.

KEY FACTS

MAJOR PARTS: (*with number of speeches/scenes on stage*) Proteus (20%/147/11), Valentine (17%/149/6), Julia (14%/107/7), Speed (9%/117/6), Lance (9%/68/4), Duke (9%/48/5), Silvia (7%/58/6), Lucetta (3%/48/2), Turio (3%/36/5).

LINGUISTIC MEDIUM: 80% verse, 20% prose. High frequency of rhyme.

DATE: Early 1590s. Mentioned by Francis Meres in 1598. Presumed on stylistic grounds to be one of the earliest plays, but no firm evidence for any particular year.

SOURCES: Main plot based on a story in Jorge de Montemayor, *Diana Enamorada* (originally in Spanish—English translation by Bartholomew Yong published 1598, but circulated in manuscript several years earlier); plot may be mediated via a lost Queen's Men play of the 1580s, *Felix and Feliomena*. Other literary influences seem to include Arthur Brooke, *Romeus and Juliet* (1562) and John Lyly, *Euphues* (1578), and perhaps *Midas* (c.1589).

TEXT: First Folio of 1623 is the only early printed text. Based on a transcript by Ralph Crane, professional scribe working for the King's Men. Generally good quality of printing.

THE TWO GENTLEMEN OF VERONA

LIST OF PARTS

VALENTINE }
PROTEUS } the two gentlemen

SPEED a clownish servant to Valentine

LANCE the like to Proteus

DUKE of Milan, father to Silvia

SILVIA beloved of Valentine

EGLAMOUR agent for Silvia in her escape

ANTONIO father to Proteus

PANTINO servant to Antonio

TURIO a foolish rival to Valentine

JULIA beloved of Proteus

LUCETTA waiting-woman to Julia

HOST where Julia lodges

OUTLAWS with Valentine

Servants, Musicians, Lance's dog Crab

List of parts **clownish servant** actually a quick-witted page boy **the like** actually older than Speed and more foolish—the role for the company clown

Act 1 Scene 1

Enter Valentine [and] Proteus

VALENTINE   Cease to persuade, my loving Proteus:
Home-keeping youth have ever homely wits.
Were't not affection chains thy tender days
To the sweet glances of thy honoured love,
5   I rather would entreat thy company
To see the wonders of the world abroad,
Than — living dully sluggardized at home —
Wear out thy youth with shapeless idleness.
But since thou lov'st, love still, and thrive therein,
10   Even as I would, when I to love begin.

PROTEUS   Wilt thou be gone? Sweet Valentine, adieu.
Think on thy Proteus, when thou haply see'st
Some rare noteworthy object in thy travel.
Wish me partaker in thy happiness
15   When thou dost meet good hap: and in thy danger —
If ever danger do environ thee —
Commend thy grievance to my holy prayers,
For I will be thy beadsman, Valentine.

VALENTINE   And on a love-book pray for my success?
20   PROTEUS   Upon some book I love, I'll pray for thee.
VALENTINE   That's on some shallow story of deep love:
How young Leander crossed the Hellespont.
PROTEUS   That's a deep story, of a deeper love,
For he was more than over-shoes in love.
25   VALENTINE   'Tis true: for you are over-boots in love,
And yet you never swam the Hellespont.

1.1 Location: Verona   Valentine his name signifies a lover (from the patron saint of lovers)
Proteus from the Greek god known for his ability to change shape at will; a name often used
to suggest deceit   **2 homely** simple/dull   **3 affection** love/sexual desire   **tender** youthful
7 sluggardized in a state of idleness   **8 shapeless** purposeless   **9 still** constantly   **12 haply**
by chance   **15 hap** chance   **16 environ** surround   **17 Commend thy grievance** entrust your
unhappiness   **18 beadsman** person paid to pray for others   **19 love-book** courtship manual
or tale of love   **22 Leander . . . Hellespont** in classical mythology Leander regularly swam
across the Hellespont to see his lover Hero, until one night he drowned   **24 over-shoes in love**
shoe-deep/immersed in love

	PROTEUS	Over the boots? Nay, give me not the boots.
	VALENTINE	No, I will not, for it boots thee not.
	PROTEUS	What?
30	VALENTINE	To be in love, where scorn is bought with groans:

VALENTINE To be in love, where scorn is bought with groans:
Coy looks with heart-sore sighs, one fading moment's
    mirth,
With twenty watchful, weary, tedious nights;
If haply won, perhaps a hapless gain,
If lost, why then a grievous labour won;
However, but a folly bought with wit,
Or else a wit by folly vanquishèd.

PROTEUS   So, by your circumstance, you call me fool.
VALENTINE So, by your circumstance, I fear you'll prove.
PROTEUS   'Tis Love you cavil at: I am not Love.
VALENTINE Love is your master, for he masters you:
And he that is so yokèd by a fool,
Methinks should not be chronicled for wise.

PROTEUS   Yet writers say: as in the sweetest bud
The eating canker dwells, so eating love
Inhabits in the finest wits of all.

VALENTINE And writers say: as the most forward bud
Is eaten by the canker ere it blow,
Even so by love, the young and tender wit
Is turned to folly, blasting in the bud,
Losing his verdure, even in the prime,
And all the fair effects of future hopes.
But wherefore waste I time to counsel thee
That art a votary to fond desire?

---

27 give . . . boots don't make a fool of me   28 boots profits   31 Coy disdainful   32 watchful
wakeful   33 hapless unlucky   34 If . . . won if the lover fails to win his lady then all that he
will have gained is sorrow and effort   35 However whatever the outcome   but merely
a folly foolishness   37 circumstance elaborate speech   38 circumstance situation   39 cavil
quibble/complain   Love refers here to Cupid   41 yokèd bound/controlled   42 chronicled for
recorded as being   44 eating canker worm that feeds off and destroys plants   46 forward
early   47 blow bloom   49 blasting withering   50 verdure green freshness   prime spring
51 effects outcome   52 wherefore why   counsel advise   53 votary devoted worshipper
fond foolish/doting

Once more, adieu. My father at the road
55 Expects my coming, there to see me shipped.

PROTEUS   And thither will I bring thee, Valentine.

VALENTINE   Sweet Proteus, no: now let us take our leave.
To Milan let me hear from thee by letters
Of thy success in love, and what news else
60 Betideth here in absence of thy friend:
And I likewise will visit thee with mine.

PROTEUS   All happiness bechance to thee in Milan.

VALENTINE   As much to you at home: and so, farewell.   *Exit*

PROTEUS   He after honour hunts, I after love;
65 He leaves his friends to dignify them more;
I leave myself, my friends and all, for love.
Thou, Julia, thou hast metamorphosed me:
Made me neglect my studies, lose my time,
War with good counsel, set the world at nought;
70 Made wit with musing weak, heart sick with thought.

[*Enter Speed*]

SPEED   Sir Proteus, 'save you. Saw you my master?

PROTEUS   But now he parted hence to embark for Milan.

SPEED   Twenty to one then, he is shipped already,
And I have played the sheep in losing him.

75 PROTEUS   Indeed, a sheep doth very often stray,
An if the shepherd be awhile away.

SPEED   You conclude that my master is a shepherd, then,
and I a sheep?

PROTEUS   I do.

80 SPEED   Why then, my horns are his horns, whether I wake
or sleep.

---

54 **road** harbor   55 **shipped** dispatched on board a ship   58 **Milan** northern Italian
dukedom   59 **success** destiny   60 **Betideth** takes place   61 **mine** i.e. my letters full of news
62 **bechance** happen   65 **dignify** honor (by improving his own reputation in the world)
66 **leave** abandon/neglect   67 **Julia** possibly named after the Juliet in Arthur Brooke's poem
Romeus and Juliet; her name may also signify passion, being derived from the hot month of July
69 **War** disagree   70 **musing** pondering   ***Speed*** a name suggesting quick wit; possibly ironic
in places as Speed is sometimes slow to go about his errands   71 **'save you** God save you
72 **But** just   74 **sheep** puns on "ship"   76 **An if** if   80 **my . . . horns** as he owns me my horns
belong to him (Speed implies that this makes Valentine a cuckold)

	PROTEUS	A silly answer, and fitting well a sheep.

PROTEUS   A silly answer, and fitting well a sheep.

SPEED   This proves me still a sheep.

PROTEUS   True: and thy master a shepherd.

85   SPEED   Nay, that I can deny by a circumstance.

PROTEUS   It shall go hard but I'll prove it by another.

SPEED   The shepherd seeks the sheep, and not the sheep the shepherd; but I seek my master, and my master seeks not me. Therefore I am no sheep.

90   PROTEUS   The sheep for fodder follow the shepherd, the shepherd for food follows not the sheep: thou for wages followest thy master, thy master for wages follows not thee. Therefore thou art a sheep.

SPEED   Such another proof will make me cry 'baa'.

95   PROTEUS   But dost thou hear? Gav'st thou my letter to Julia?

SPEED   Ay, sir: I, a lost-mutton, gave your letter to her, a laced-mutton, and she, a laced-mutton, gave me, a lost-mutton, nothing for my labour.

PROTEUS   Here's too small a pasture for such store of muttons.

100   SPEED   If the ground be overcharged, you were best stick her.

PROTEUS   Nay, in that you are astray: 'twere best pound you.

SPEED   Nay, sir, less than a pound shall serve me for carrying your letter.

105   PROTEUS   You mistake: I mean the pound — a pinfold.

SPEED   From a pound to a pin? Fold it over and over, 'tis threefold too little for carrying a letter to your lover.   *Speed*

PROTEUS   But what said she?   *Nods his head*

SPEED   Ay.

110   PROTEUS   Nod — ay — why, that's 'noddy'.

---

85 circumstance reasoned argument   **86 It . . . another** it'll be unfortunate if I can't prove the point with a different explanation   **90 fodder** food   **94 baa** puns on the contemptuous "bah"   **96 mutton** sheep   **97 laced-mutton** a prostitute wearing either lace or a tightly laced bodice   **99 store** great quantity   **100 overcharged** overcrowded   **stick** slaughter/have sex with   **102 astray** wandering into error (puns on the idea of "a stray sheep")   **pound** confine in an animal pound/beat   **103 pound** reference to money, though still punning on a beating   **105 pinfold** animal pen   **106 pin** insignificant amount   **Fold** multiply (puns on **pinfold**) with additional suggestions of folding a letter   **110 'noddy'** fool

SPEED   You mistook, sir: I say she did nod, and you ask me
if she did nod, and I say 'ay'.

PROTEUS   And that set together is noddy.

SPEED   Now you have taken the pains to set it together, take
115   it for your pains.

PROTEUS   No, no, you shall have it for bearing the letter.

SPEED   Well, I perceive I must be fain to bear with you.

PROTEUS   Why sir, how do you bear with me?

SPEED   Marry, sir, the letter, very orderly, having nothing
120   but the word 'noddy' for my pains.

PROTEUS   Beshrew me, but you have a quick wit.

SPEED   And yet it cannot overtake your slow purse.

PROTEUS   Come come, open the matter in brief: what said she?

SPEED   Open your purse, that the money and the matter
125   may be both at once delivered.

PROTEUS   Well, sir: here is for your pains. What said   *Gives*
she?   *a coin*

SPEED   Truly, sir, I think you'll hardly win her.   *Examines coin,*

PROTEUS   Why? Couldst thou perceive so much   *with contempt*
130   from her?

SPEED   Sir, I could perceive nothing at all from her; no, not
so much as a ducat for delivering your letter. And being so
hard to me that brought your mind, I fear she'll prove as
hard to you in telling your mind. Give her no token but
135   stones, for she's as hard as steel.

PROTEUS   What said she, nothing?

SPEED   No, not so much as 'Take this for thy pains.' To
testify your bounty, I thank you, you have testerned me; in

---

114 take . . . pains have it as a reward for the trouble you have taken   **117 fain to bear** obliged
to put up (with suggestions of carrying on behalf of)   **119 Marry** by the Virgin Mary   **orderly**
dutifully/properly   **121 Beshrew** the devil take   **123 open the matter** reveal the information
128 hardly with great difficulty   **129 perceive** understand/glean   **131 perceive** receive (may
play on **purse**)   **132 ducat** gold coin   **133 brought your mind** conveyed your feelings to her
134 in . . . mind when you tell her of your emotions in person   **token** lover's gift   **135 stones**
jewels   **138 bounty** generosity   **testerned me** given me sixpence (a "testern")

140   requital whereof, henceforth carry your letters yourself. And
so, sir, I'll commend you to my master.

PROTEUS   Go, go, begone, to save your ship from wreck,

                                                [Exit Speed]

Which cannot perish having thee aboard,
Being destined to a drier death on shore.
I must go send some better messenger:

145   I fear my Julia would not deign my lines,
Receiving them from such a worthless post.   Exit

Act 1 Scene 2   *running scene 2*

Enter Julia and Lucetta

JULIA   But say, Lucetta — now we are alone —
Wouldst thou then counsel me to fall in love?

LUCETTA   Ay, madam, so you stumble not unheedfully.

JULIA   Of all the fair resort of gentlemen

5   That every day with parle encounter me,
In thy opinion, which is worthiest love?

LUCETTA   Please you repeat their names, I'll show my mind,
According to my shallow simple skill.

JULIA   What think'st thou of the fair Sir Eglamour?

10   LUCETTA   As of a knight well-spoken, neat and fine;
But, were I you, he never should be mine.

JULIA   What think'st thou of the rich Mercatio?

LUCETTA   Well of his wealth; but of himself, so so.

JULIA   What think'st thou of the gentle Proteus?

15   LUCETTA   Lord, Lord: to see what folly reigns in us!

JULIA   How now? What means this passion at his name?

---

139 requital whereof return for which   **140 commend** present greetings from   **141 begone**
go away (expression of annoyance)   **143 drier death** i.e. hanging   **145 deign my lines** accept
my letter   **146 post** messenger/idiot   **1.2** *Lucetta* diminutive form of "Lucy"   **3 so**
providing that   **stumble** trip/have sex   **unheedfully** carelessly/recklessly   **4 resort** company
5 parle talk   **9 Sir Eglamour** almost certainly a different Eglamour from the one who appears
later in the play; *amor* is Latin for "love"   **10 neat** elegant   **12 Mercatio** his name suggests
that he is a merchant   **14 gentle** well-born/honorable   **16 passion** outburst

LUCETTA   Pardon, dear madam: 'tis a passing shame
That I — unworthy body as I am —
Should censure thus on lovely gentlemen.

20 JULIA   Why not on Proteus, as of all the rest?

LUCETTA   Then thus: of many good, I think him best.

JULIA   Your reason?

LUCETTA   I have no other, but a woman's reason:
I think him so because I think him so.

25 JULIA   And wouldst thou have me cast my love on him?

LUCETTA   Ay, if you thought your love not cast away.

JULIA   Why he, of all the rest, hath never moved me.

LUCETTA   Yet he, of all the rest, I think best loves ye.

JULIA   His little speaking shows his love but small.

30 LUCETTA   Fire that's closest kept burns most of all.

JULIA   They do not love that do not show their love.

LUCETTA   O, they love least that let men know their love.

JULIA   I would I knew his mind.

LUCETTA   Peruse this paper, madam.   *Gives a letter*

35 JULIA   'To Julia'. Say, from whom?

LUCETTA   That the contents will show.

JULIA   Say, say: who gave it thee?

LUCETTA   Sir Valentine's page: and sent, I think, from Proteus.
He would have given it you, but I, being in the way,
40 Did in your name receive it: pardon the fault, I pray.

JULIA   Now, by my modesty, a goodly broker!
Dare you presume to harbour wanton lines?
To whisper and conspire against my youth?
Now trust me, 'tis an office of great worth,
45 And you an officer fit for the place.
There, take the paper: see it be returned,
Or else return no more into my sight.

LUCETTA   To plead for love deserves more fee than hate.

---

17 passing surpassing, extreme (puns on **passion**)   **19 censure** pass judgment on   **25 cast** bestow   **26 cast away** wasted   **27 moved** wooed   **29 little speaking** very few words on the subject   **39 being . . . it** happening to meet him I took the letter on your behalf   **41 goodly broker** fine intermediary   **42 wanton** passionate/lewd   **44 office** position   **48 fee** recompense

JULIA   Will ye be gone?

50   LUCETTA   That you may ruminate.   *Exit*

JULIA   And yet I would I had o'erlooked the letter;
It were a shame to call her back again
And pray her to a fault for which I chid her.
What fool is she, that knows I am a maid,
55   And would not force the letter to my view!
Since maids, in modesty, say 'no' to that
Which they would have the profferer construe 'ay'.
Fie, fie: how wayward is this foolish love
That — like a testy babe — will scratch the nurse
60   And presently, all humbled, kiss the rod!
How churlishly I chid Lucetta hence,
When willingly I would have had her here!
How angerly I taught my brow to frown,
When inward joy enforced my heart to smile!
65   My penance is to call Lucetta back
And ask remission for my folly past.
What ho! Lucetta!

[*Enter Lucetta*]

LUCETTA   What would your ladyship?

JULIA   Is't near dinner-time?

70   LUCETTA   I would it were,
That you might kill your stomach on your meat
And not upon your maid.   *Drops a letter,*

JULIA   What is't that you took up so gingerly?   *then picks it up*

LUCETTA   Nothing.

75   JULIA   Why didst thou stoop then?

LUCETTA   To take a paper up that I let fall.

JULIA   And is that paper nothing?

---

50 That . . . ruminate (yes) in order to enable you to think   **51 I had o'erlooked** I wish I had
read   **53 pray her to** beg her to commit   **chid** rebuked   **57 have . . . 'ay'** rather the person
making the offer interpreted as "yes"   **58 wayward** perverse, unreasonable   **59 testy** irritable
60 presently immediately   **kiss the rod** be obedient   **rod** cane   **61 churlishly** roughly,
ungraciously   **63 angerly** angrily   **66 remission** forgiveness   **71 kill your stomach** satisfy
your appetite/calm your bad temper (**meat** was pronounced "mate" and thus puns on **maid**)

	LUCETTA	Nothing concerning me.
	JULIA	Then let it lie for those that it concerns.
80	LUCETTA	Madam, it will not lie where it concerns,

LUCETTA Nothing concerning me.

JULIA Then let it lie for those that it concerns.

80   LUCETTA Madam, it will not lie where it concerns,
Unless it have a false interpreter.

JULIA Some love of yours hath writ to you in rhyme.

LUCETTA That I might sing it, madam, to a tune.
Give me a note: your ladyship can set—

85   JULIA As little by such toys as may be possible.
Best sing it to the tune of 'Light o'love'.

LUCETTA It is too heavy for so light a tune.

JULIA Heavy? Belike it hath some burden then?

LUCETTA Ay, and melodious were it, would you sing it.

90   JULIA And why not you?

LUCETTA I cannot reach so high.

JULIA Let's see your song.   *Takes the letter*
How now, minion!

LUCETTA Keep tune there still, so you will sing it out:
And yet methinks I do not like this tune.

95   JULIA You do not?

LUCETTA No, madam, 'tis too sharp.

JULIA You, minion, are too saucy.

LUCETTA Nay, now you are too flat,
And mar the concord with too harsh a descant:

100 There wanteth but a mean to fill your song.

JULIA The mean is drowned with your unruly bass.

LUCETTA Indeed, I bid the base for Proteus.

---

79 let . . . concerns leave it there for those it is intended for   **80 lie . . . concerns** fib about its contents   **81 false interpreter** untrustworthy/untrue reader   **83 That** in order that   **84 set** set to music (in the next line Julia intends the sense of "set store by")   **85 toys** trifles   **86 'Light o' love'** a popular tune   **87 heavy** serious/burdensome   **light** frivolous/of little weight   **88 burden** bass accompaniment/chorus/**heavy** load   **91 reach so high** sing at such a high pitch/win someone of Proteus' status   **92 minion** minx, mischievous one   **93 tune** melody/temper   **so . . . out** in that way you will finish the song/rid yourself of your mood   **96 sharp** shrill/cross   **98 flat** tunelessly low in pitch/blunt   **99 mar** spoil   **concord** harmony   **descant** harmonious variation on the tune   **100 mean** middle point/method/tenor (a male voice—i.e. that of Proteus)   **101 unruly bass** uncontrolled bass voice/unworthy, low behavior   **102 bid the base** sing the male part/challenge to a chase

JULIA   This babble shall not henceforth trouble me.
             Here is a coil with protestation!   *Tears the letter*

105   Go, get you gone, and let the papers lie:
       You would be fing'ring them to anger me.

LUCETTA   She makes it strange, but she would be best pleased
             To be so angered with another letter.   [*Exit*]

JULIA   Nay, would I were so angered with the same:
110   O hateful hands, to tear such loving words;
       Injurious wasps, to feed on such sweet honey
       And kill the bees that yield it with your stings!
       I'll kiss each several paper for amends.
       Look, here is writ 'kind Julia'. Unkind Julia,   ↓*Examining the pieces*↓
115   As in revenge of thy ingratitude,
       I throw thy name against the bruising stones,
       Trampling contemptuously on thy disdain.
       And here is writ 'love-wounded Proteus'.
       Poor wounded name: my bosom as a bed
120   Shall lodge thee till thy wound be throughly healed;
       And thus I search it with a sovereign kiss.
       But twice or thrice was 'Proteus' written down.
       Be calm, good wind, blow not a word away
       Till I have found each letter, in the letter,
125   Except mine own name: that, some whirlwind bear
       Unto a ragged, fearful, hanging rock,
       And throw it thence into the raging sea.
       Lo, here in one line is his name twice writ:
       'Poor forlorn Proteus, passionate Proteus,
130   To the sweet Julia': that I'll tear away:

---

104 coil with protestation fuss about declarations of love   **106 fing'ring** fiddling with/stealing
107 makes it strange pretends she doesn't care   **109 would . . . same** I wish that I had the
letter back to be able to appear enraged by it/I wish that it really was anger that I was feeling
about the letter   **111 Injurious wasps** unjust/harmful wasps (i.e. fingers)   **113 several paper**
scrap of the torn-up letter   **114 Unkind** cruel/unnatural   **115 As** as if   **119 my . . . thee** I
shall keep the scrap of paper with your name on it in my breast pocket/my heart will nurture
your name   **120 throughly** thoroughly   **121 search** clean/probe (a wound)   **sovereign**
healing   **126 ragged** rugged   **130 that** i.e. the part with her name on it

And yet I will not, sith so prettily
He couples it to his complaining names.
Thus will I fold them, one upon another;
Now kiss, embrace, contend, do what you will.

[Enter Lucetta]

135 LUCETTA   Madam, dinner is ready, and your father stays.

JULIA   Well, let us go.

LUCETTA   What, shall these papers lie like tell-tales here?

JULIA   If you respect them, best to take them up.

LUCETTA   Nay, I was taken up for laying them down.

140   Yet here they shall not lie, for catching cold.   *Picks up the pieces*

JULIA   I see you have a month's mind to them.

LUCETTA   Ay, madam, you may say what sights you see;
I see things too, although you judge I wink.

JULIA   Come, come: will't please you go?   *Exeunt*

Act 1 Scene 3   *running scene 3*

Enter Antonio and Pantino

ANTONIO   Tell me, Pantino, what sad talk was that
Wherewith my brother held you in the cloister?

PANTINO   'Twas of his nephew Proteus, your son.

ANTONIO   Why? What of him?

5 PANTINO   He wondered that your lordship
Would suffer him to spend his youth at home,
While other men, of slender reputation,
Put forth their sons to seek preferment out:
Some to the wars to try their fortune there,

131 **sith** since   132 **He . . . names** he links my name to his lamenting one   133 **Thus . . . another** Julia folds the paper so that her name is lying upon that of Proteus (the sexual nature of this is continued in the following line in which the actions described become increasingly physical)   134 **contend** grapple, engage with sexually   135 **stays** waits   138 **respect** value   139 **taken up** rebuked   140 **for** lest they should   141 **month's mind to** preference for   143 **judge I wink** think my eyes are shut   **1.3** *Pantino* possibly from "pantler," a type of servant, and the Italian diminutive *ino*   1 **sad** serious   2 **cloister** covered arcade adjoining a building   6 **suffer** allow   7 **slender reputation** lesser/insignificant status/repute   8 **Put forth** send out into the world   **preferment** advancement, favor

10   Some to discover islands far away,
      Some to the studious universities;
      For any or for all these exercises,
      He said that Proteus your son was meet,
      And did request me to importune you
15   To let him spend his time no more at home,
      Which would be great impeachment to his age,
      In having known no travel in his youth.

ANTONIO   Nor need'st thou much importune me to that
      Whereon this month I have been hammering.
20   I have considered well his loss of time,
      And how he cannot be a perfect man,
      Not being tried and tutored in the world:
      Experience is by industry achieved
      And perfected by the swift course of time.
25   Then tell me, whither were I best to send him?

PANTINO   I think your lordship is not ignorant
      How his companion, youthful Valentine,
      Attends the emperor in his royal court.

ANTONIO   I know it well.

30   PANTINO   'Twere good, I think, your lordship sent him thither:
      There shall he practise tilts and tournaments,
      Hear sweet discourse, converse with noblemen,
      And be in eye of every exercise
      Worthy his youth and nobleness of birth.

35   ANTONIO   I like thy counsel: well hast thou advised.
      And that thou mayst perceive how well I like it,
      The execution of it shall make known.
      Even with the speediest expedition
      I will dispatch him to the emperor's court.

---

13 meet suitable   14 importune urge   16 impeachment . . . age discredit to him when
he is older   19 hammering thinking hard about   21 perfect complete/fully rounded and
experienced   22 tried tested   26 ignorant unaware   28 emperor the Duke of Milan—he is
referred to as both "emperor" and "duke" in the play   31 practise tilts take part in jousts
32 sweet discourse elegant conversation   33 in eye of witness to   37 execution carrying out
38 expedition haste

40   PANTINO   Tomorrow, may it please you, Don Alfonso
            With other gentlemen of good esteem
            Are journeying to salute the emperor
            And to commend their service to his will.
      ANTONIO   Good company: with them shall Proteus go.
      [*Enter Proteus, reading*]
45   And in good time! Now will we break with him.
      PROTEUS   Sweet love, sweet lines, sweet life!
            Here is her hand, the agent of her heart;
            Here is her oath for love, her honour's pawn.
            O, that our fathers would applaud our loves
50   To seal our happiness with their consents.
            O heavenly Julia!
      ANTONIO   How now? What letter are you reading there?
      PROTEUS   May't please your lordship, 'tis a word or two
            Of commendations sent from Valentine,
55   Delivered by a friend that came from him.
      ANTONIO   Lend me the letter: let me see what news.
      PROTEUS   There is no news, my lord, but that he writes
            How happily he lives, how well beloved
            And daily gracèd by the emperor,
60   Wishing me with him, partner of his fortune.
      ANTONIO   And how stand you affected to his wish?
      PROTEUS   As one relying on your lordship's will,
            And not depending on his friendly wish.
      ANTONIO   My will is something sorted with his wish.
65   Muse not that I thus suddenly proceed:
            For what I will, I will, and there an end.
            I am resolved that thou shalt spend some time
            With Valentinus in the emperor's court:
            What maintenance he from his friends receives,

---

43 **commend** commit   45 **in good time** just at the right moment   **break with** reveal the plan
to   47 **hand** handwriting   48 **pawn** pledge   50 **seal** ratify/complete   54 **commendations**
greeting   59 **gracèd** favored   61 **stand you affected** are you inclined   63 **his** i.e. Valentine's
64 **something sorted** somewhat in agreement   65 **Muse** wonder   69 **maintenance** allowance
friends supporters/relatives

70   Like exhibition thou shalt have from me.
      Tomorrow be in readiness to go:
      Excuse it not, for I am peremptory.
PROTEUS   My lord, I cannot be so soon provided:
      Please you deliberate a day or two.
75 ANTONIO   Look what thou want'st shall be sent after thee.
      No more of stay: tomorrow thou must go.
      Come on, Pantino, you shall be employed
      To hasten on his expedition.   [*Exeunt Antonio and Pantino*]
PROTEUS   Thus have I shunned the fire for fear of burning,
80   And drenched me in the sea where I am drowned.
      I feared to show my father Julia's letter,
      Lest he should take exceptions to my love,
      And with the vantage of mine own excuse
      Hath he excepted most against my love.
85   O, how this spring of love resembleth
      The uncertain glory of an April day,
      Which now shows all the beauty of the sun,
      And by and by a cloud takes all away.
    [*Enter Pantino*]
PANTINO   Sir Proteus, your father calls for you:
90   He is in haste, therefore I pray you go.
PROTEUS   Why, this it is: my heart accords thereto,
      And yet a thousand times it answers 'no'.   *Exeunt*

Act 2 Scene 1   *running scene 4*

    Enter Valentine [and] Speed

SPEED   Sir, your glove.
VALENTINE   Not mine: my gloves are on.
SPEED   Why then, this may be yours, for this is but one.

70 **Like exhibition** the same amount   72 **Excuse it not** make no excuses   **peremptory**
resolved   73 **provided** equipped   75 **Look** see that   76 **No . . . stay** no further talk of
lingering   82 **take exceptions** make objections   83 **vantage** benefit   84 **excepted most**
against caused the greatest obstacle to   91 **accords** agrees   **2.1 *Location: Milan***   2 **on**
pronounced "one" (thus allowing for the pun in the following line)

VALENTINE   Ha! Let me see: ay, give it me, it's mine.

5   Sweet ornament that decks a thing divine.

          Ah, Silvia, Silvia!

SPEED   Madam Silvia! Madam Silvia!   *Calls*

VALENTINE   How now, sirrah?

SPEED   She is not within hearing, sir.

10   VALENTINE   Why, sir, who bade you call her?

SPEED   Your worship, sir, or else I mistook.

VALENTINE   Well, you'll still be too forward.

SPEED   And yet I was last chidden for being too slow.

VALENTINE   Go to, sir: tell me, do you know Madam Silvia?

15   SPEED   She that your worship loves?

VALENTINE   Why, how know you that I am in love?

SPEED   Marry, by these special marks: first, you have
          learned — like Sir Proteus — to wreathe your arms like a
          malcontent: to relish a love-song like a robin-redbreast: to
20   walk alone like one that had the pestilence: to sigh like a
          school-boy that had lost his A B C: to weep like a young
          wench that had buried her grandam: to fast like one that
          takes diet: to watch like one that fears robbing: to speak
          puling like a beggar at Hallowmas. You were wont, when you
25   laughed, to crow like a cock: when you walked, to walk like
          one of the lions: when you fasted, it was presently after
          dinner: when you looked sadly, it was for want of money.
          And now you are metamorphosed with a mistress, that,
          when I look on you, I can hardly think you my master.

30   VALENTINE   Are all these things perceived in me?

SPEED   They are all perceived without ye.

---

5 ornament item of clothing   decks adorns   6 Silvia from the Latin "silva" meaning
"woods"; also signifies a woodland deity or spirit   8 sirrah sir (authoritative)   12 still always
forward hasty/lively   14 Go to expression of dismissive impatience   17 special marks
particular signs   18 wreathe fold (considered a sign of melancholy)   19 malcontent
discontented person   relish sing/have a taste for/enjoy   20 pestilence plague (victims were
shunned for fear of infection)   21 lost his A B C lost his schoolbook/forgotten the alphabet
22 grandam grandmother   23 watch remain awake   24 puling whiningly   beggar at
Hallowmas beggars traditionally made special requests for aid on All Saints' Day (1 November)
wont accustomed previously   26 presently immediately   27 want lack   31 without ye
externally

VALENTINE   Without me? They cannot.

SPEED   Without you? Nay, that's certain: for, without you
were so simple, none else would. But you are so without
35   these follies, that these follies are within you, and shine
through you like the water in an urinal, that not an eye that
sees you but is a physician to comment on your malady.

VALENTINE   But tell me, dost thou know my lady Silvia?

SPEED   She that you gaze on so, as she sits at supper?

40   VALENTINE   Hast thou observed that? Even she, I mean.

SPEED   Why sir, I know her not.

VALENTINE   Dost thou know her by my gazing on her, and yet
know'st her not?

SPEED   Is she not hard-favoured, sir?

45   VALENTINE   Not so fair, boy, as well-favoured.

SPEED   Sir, I know that well enough.

VALENTINE   What dost thou know?

SPEED   That she is not so fair as, of you, well-favoured.

VALENTINE   I mean that her beauty is exquisite, but her favour
50   infinite.

SPEED   That's because the one is painted and the other out
of all count.

VALENTINE   How painted? And how out of count?

SPEED   Marry, sir, so painted to make her fair, that no man
55   counts of her beauty.

VALENTINE   How esteem'st thou me? I account of her beauty.

SPEED   You never saw her since she was deformed.

VALENTINE   How long hath she been deformed?

SPEED   Ever since you loved her.

60   VALENTINE   I have loved her ever since I saw her, and still I see
her beautiful.

---

32 Without me out of my presence   **33 without** unless   **35 you . . . you** you surround these
follies so fully that they are visible within you/you are so simple that even without these
external signs of folly your internal folly would shine through   **36 water . . . urinal** urine in a
glass vessel used by doctors for diagnosis   **37 malady** illness   **40 Even she** herself   **44 hard-
favoured** ugly   **45 well-favoured** attractive/gracious   **48 of you, well-favoured** preferred by
you   **49 favour** good will/charm   **51 painted** artificial (painted on with cosmetics)   **out . . .
count** beyond calculation   **55 counts of** esteems, values   **56 How . . . me?** i.e. Do you think
nothing, then, of my judgment?   **57 deformed** disfigured/transformed by love in Valentine's
eyes

SPEED   If you love her, you cannot see her.

VALENTINE   Why?

SPEED   Because Love is blind. O, that you had mine eyes, or
65   your own eyes had the lights they were wont to have when
      you chid at Sir Proteus for going ungartered!

VALENTINE   What should I see then?

SPEED   Your own present folly and her passing deformity:
      for he, being in love, could not see to garter his hose; and you,
70   being in love, cannot see to put on your hose.

VALENTINE   Belike, boy, then you are in love, for last morning
      you could not see to wipe my shoes.

SPEED   True, sir: I was in love with my bed. I thank you, you
      swinged me for my love, which makes me the bolder to chide
75   you for yours.

VALENTINE   In conclusion, I stand affected to her.

SPEED   I would you were set, so your affection would cease.

VALENTINE   Last night she enjoined me to write some lines to
      one she loves.

80   SPEED   And have you?

VALENTINE   I have.

SPEED   Are they not lamely writ?

VALENTINE   No, boy, but as well as I can do them.
      Peace! Here she comes.

85   SPEED   O, excellent motion! O, exceeding   *Aside*
      puppet! Now will he interpret to her.

[*Enter Silvia*]

VALENTINE   Madam and mistress, a thousand good-morrows.

SPEED   O, 'give ye good ev'n: here's a million of   *Aside*
      manners.

SILVIA   Sir Valentine and servant, to you two thousand.

---

64 **Love is blind** Cupid was traditionally depicted as blind   65 **lights** clear-sightedness
66 **ungartered** with his garters undone (i.e. disheveled, traditionally a sign of one in love)
69 **hose** breeches (Valentine is in an even worse condition than Proteus, who at least managed
to put on his hose)   74 **swinged** beat   76 **stand affected to** love (in his reply, Speed plays on
the sense of **stand** as "have an erection")   77 **set** calm/seated   85 **motion** puppet show
86 **interpret to her** provide the words for the puppet (Silvia)   88 **'give . . . ev'n** God give you a
plain "good evening" (instead of these elaborate greetings)   **million of** excessive quantity
89 **servant** a lover who served and was devoted to his lady

90   SPEED   He should give her interest, and she gives   *Aside*
    it him.

VALENTINE   As you enjoined me, I have writ your letter
    Unto the secret, nameless friend of yours,
    Which I was much unwilling to proceed in
    But for my duty to your ladyship.   *Gives her a letter*

95   SILVIA   I thank you, gentle servant: 'tis very clerkly done.

VALENTINE   Now trust me, madam, it came hardly off:
    For being ignorant to whom it goes
    I writ at random, very doubtfully.

SILVIA   Perchance you think too much of so much pains?

100   VALENTINE   No, madam, so it stead you, I will write —
    Please you command — a thousand times as much.
    And yet—

SILVIA   A pretty period! Well, I guess the sequel,
    And yet I will not name it: and yet I care not.
105   And yet take this again. And yet I thank you,   *Offers him the letter*
    Meaning henceforth to trouble you no more.

SPEED   And yet you will, and yet another 'yet'.   *Aside*

VALENTINE   What means your ladyship? Do you not like it?

SILVIA   Yes, yes: the lines are very quaintly writ,
110   But, since unwillingly, take them again.   *Offers the letter again*
    Nay, take them.

VALENTINE   Madam, they are for you.

SILVIA   Ay, ay: you writ them, sir, at my request,
    But I will none of them. They are for you:
115   I would have had them writ more movingly.

VALENTINE   Please you, I'll write your ladyship another.

SILVIA   And when it's writ, for my sake read it over,
    And if it please you, so: if not, why, so.

---

90 He . . . him as her lover, Valentine should express personal interest in Silvia, yet she gives
him financial interest by doubling the number of greetings he has given her   92 friend lover
95 clerkly scholarly   96 came hardly off was accomplished with difficulty   98 doubtfully
hesitantly   99 Perchance . . . pains perhaps you think it is not worth making so much effort
100 so . . . you as long as it is of help to you   103 pretty period fine/clever pause/conclusion
the sequel what was to come next   105 this i.e. the letter   109 quaintly skillfully   110 again
back   114 none of have nothing to do with   118 so so be it

	VALENTINE	If it please me, madam? What then?
120	SILVIA	Why, if it please you, take it for your labour;
		And so, good morrow, servant. *Exit*
	SPEED	O, jest unseen, inscrutable, invisible *Aside*
		As a nose on a man's face, or a weathercock on a steeple!
		My master sues to her, and she hath taught her suitor,
125		He being her pupil, to become her tutor.
		O, excellent device! Was there ever heard a better?
		That my master, being scribe,
		To himself should write the letter?
	VALENTINE	How now, sir? What, are you reasoning with
		yourself?
130	SPEED	Nay, I was rhyming: 'tis you that have the reason.
	VALENTINE	To do what?
	SPEED	To be a spokesman from Madam Silvia.
	VALENTINE	To whom?
	SPEED	To yourself: why, she woos you by a figure.
135	VALENTINE	What figure?
	SPEED	By a letter, I should say.
	VALENTINE	Why, she hath not writ to me?
	SPEED	What need she, when she hath made you write to
		yourself? Why, do you not perceive the jest?
140	VALENTINE	No, believe me.
	SPEED	No believing you indeed, sir. But did you perceive
		her earnest?
	VALENTINE	She gave me none, except an angry word.
	SPEED	Why, she hath given you a letter.
145	VALENTINE	That's the letter I writ to her friend.
	SPEED	And that letter hath she delivered, and there an end.
	VALENTINE	I would it were no worse.
	SPEED	I'll warrant you, 'tis as well:
		For often have you writ to her, and she in modesty,

---

120 for your labour as payment for your efforts   **124 sues to** pleads with/courts   **126 device**
scheme/invention   **129 reasoning** talking/debating   **134 figure** ingenious device/number
142 earnest to be serious (the following line plays on the sense of "financial deposit")
143 none nothing   **146 end** end to the matter/purpose   **148 warrant** assure

150   Or else for want of idle time, could not again reply,
        Or fearing else some messenger that might her mind
            discover,
        Herself hath taught her love himself to write unto her lover.
        All this I speak in print, for in print I found it.
        Why muse you, sir? 'Tis dinner-time.
155   VALENTINE   I have dined.
        SPEED   Ay, but hearken, sir: though the chameleon Love
        can feed on the air, I am one that am nourished by my
        victuals, and would fain have meat. O, be not like your
        mistress: be moved, be moved.   *Exeunt*

Act 2 Scene 2   *running scene 5*

Enter Proteus [and] Julia

        PROTEUS   Have patience, gentle Julia.
        JULIA   I must, where is no remedy.
        PROTEUS   When possibly I can, I will return.
        JULIA   If you turn not, you will return the sooner.
5   Keep this remembrance for thy Julia's sake.   *Gives a ring*
        PROTEUS   Why then, we'll make exchange; here,   *Gives a ring*
            take you this.
        JULIA   And seal the bargain with a holy kiss.   *They kiss*
        PROTEUS   Here is my hand for my true constancy:
        And when that hour o'erslips me in the day,
10   Wherein I sigh not, Julia, for thy sake,
        The next ensuing hour some foul mischance
        Torment me for my love's forgetfulness.
        My father stays my coming: answer not,

---

150 **want** lack   151 **discover** reveal   153 **in print** very precisely, as if quoting from a book
155 **I have dined** implying that he has feasted upon Silvia's looks   156 **chameleon . . . air** Love
was supposed to be changeable, like the chameleon, a creature that can alter its color and that
was reputed to survive on air   158 **victuals** food   **fain** willingly   159 **moved** sympathetic/
persuaded to go to dinner   **2.2 Location: Verona**   2 **is** there is   4 **turn** change, become
unfaithful   5 **remembrance** love token, keepsake   8 **constancy** fidelity   9 **o'erslips** passes by
unnoticed   11 **mischance** misfortune   13 **stays** awaits

The tide is now; nay, not thy tide of tears,

15   That tide will stay me longer than I should.

Julia, farewell. What, gone without a word?   [*Exit Julia*]

Ay, so true love should do: it cannot speak,

For truth hath better deeds than words to grace it.

[*Enter Pantino*]

PANTINO   Sir Proteus, you are stayed for.

20 PROTEUS   Go: I come, I come.

Alas, this parting strikes poor lovers dumb.   *Exeunt*

Act 2 Scene 3

running scene 6

Enter Lance [leading his dog, Crab]

LANCE   Nay, 'twill be this hour ere I have done weeping: all the kind of the Lances have this very fault. I have received my proportion, like the prodigious son, and am going with Sir Proteus to the Imperial's court. I think Crab, my dog, be

5 the sourest-natured dog that lives: my mother weeping, my father wailing, my sister crying, our maid howling, our cat wringing her hands, and all our house in a great perplexity, yet did not this cruel-hearted cur shed one tear: he is a stone, a very pebble stone, and has no more pity in him than a dog.

10 A Jew would have wept to have seen our parting. Why, my grandam, having no eyes, look you, wept herself blind at my parting. Nay, I'll show you the manner of it. This shoe is my father. No, this left shoe is my father. No, no, this left shoe is my mother. Nay, that cannot be so neither. Yes, it is so, it is so:

15 it hath the worser sole. This shoe with the hole in it is my mother, and this my father. A vengeance on't, there 'tis.

---

15 stay detain   **18 grace** adorn/do honor to   **2.3**   *Lance* short form of Lancelot; the name may also be derived from the Old French *l'ancelot* ("attendant")   **1 ere** before   **2 kind** family **3 proportion** malapropism for "portion" (i.e. "allowance")   **prodigious** malapropism for "prodigal," a reference to the well-known Bible story   **4 Imperial's** emperor's   **Crab** from "crab-apple," a sour fruit   **8 cur** dog   **10 Jew** considered to be pitiless   **12 manner of it** way it happened   **shoe** Lance uses his shoes to represent his parents   **13 left** thought to be inferior to the right   **15 sole** puns on "soul" (women supposedly had souls inferior to those of men) **hole** plays on the sense of "vagina"   **16 A vengeance on't** a mild oath: Lance is struggling to remove his shoe

Now, sir, this staff is my sister, for, look you, she is as white as
a lily and as small as a wand. This hat is Nan, our maid. I am
the dog: no, the dog is himself, and I am the dog. O, the dog is
20   me, and I am myself. Ay, so, so. Now come I to my father.
Father, your blessing: now should not the shoe speak a word
for weeping. Now should I kiss my father: well, he weeps on.
Now come I to my mother: O, that she could speak now like a
wood woman! Well, I kiss her. Why, there 'tis; here's my
25   mother's breath up and down. Now come I to my sister;
mark the moan she makes. Now the dog all this while sheds
not a tear nor speaks a word: but see how I lay the dust with
my tears.

[*Enter Pantino*]

PANTINO   Lance, away, away: aboard! Thy master is shipped,
30   and thou art to post after with oars. What's the matter? Why
weep'st thou, man? Away, ass, you'll lose the tide, if you
tarry any longer.

LANCE   It is no matter if the tied were lost, for it is the
unkindest tied that ever any man tied.

35   PANTINO   What's the unkindest tide?

LANCE   Why, he that's tied here, Crab, my dog.

PANTINO   Tut, man, I mean thou'lt lose the flood, and in
losing the flood, lose thy voyage, and in losing thy voyage,
lose thy master, and in losing thy master, lose thy service,
40   and in losing thy service— Why dost thou stop   *Lance gestures*
my mouth?   *for him to stop*

LANCE   For fear thou shouldst lose thy tongue.

PANTINO   Where should I lose my tongue?

LANCE   In thy tale.

45   PANTINO   In thy tail!

LANCE   Lose the tide, and the voyage, and the master, and
the service, and the tied! Why, man, if the river were dry, I am

---

17 staff tall walking stick   **18 small** slim   **wand** slender stick   **21 your** i.e. I ask for your
24 wood mad (playing on the fact that Lance's shoe is wooden)   **25 mother's breath** Lance is
smelling the shoe   **up and down** in every way/exactly   **26 mark** note   **27 lay the dust**
dampen the dust underfoot   **30 post** hasten   **31 lose** miss   **33 tied** i.e. Crab (puns on **tide**)
37 flood sea's tide   **42 lose** lose/loosen   **44 tale** talk, story   **45 tail** anus

able to fill it with my tears: if the wind were down, I could
drive the boat with my sighs.

50 PANTINO   Come: come away, man. I was sent to call thee.

LANCE   Sir, call me what thou dar'st.

PANTINO   Wilt thou go?

LANCE   Well, I will go.   *Exeunt*

Act 2 Scene 4   *running scene 7*

Enter Valentine, Silvia, Turio [and] Speed

SILVIA   Servant!

VALENTINE   Mistress?

SPEED   Master, Sir Turio frowns on you.

VALENTINE   Ay, boy, it's for love.

5   SPEED   Not of you.

VALENTINE   Of my mistress, then.

SPEED   'Twere good you knocked him.   *[Exit]*

SILVIA   Servant, you are sad.

VALENTINE   Indeed, madam, I seem so.

10   TURIO   Seem you that you are not?

VALENTINE   Haply I do.

TURIO   So do counterfeits.

VALENTINE   So do you.

TURIO   What seem I that I am not?

15   VALENTINE   Wise.

TURIO   What instance of the contrary?

VALENTINE   Your folly.

TURIO   And how quote you my folly?

VALENTINE   I quote it in your jerkin.

20   TURIO   My jerkin is a doublet.

VALENTINE   Well, then, I'll double your folly.

TURIO   How?

---

50 call summon   **2.4 *Location: Milan   Turio*** Latin for "sprig, young shoot," perhaps
suggesting the character's immaturity   **7 'Twere . . . knocked** it would be a good idea to hit
10 that what   **12 counterfeits** fakes, impostors   **16 instance** evidence   **18 quote** observe
(pronounced like "coat," this plays on **jerkin** in the next line)   **19 jerkin** jacket worn over a
doublet   20 doublet close-fitting jacket   **22 How?** What?

SILVIA	What, angry, Sir Turio? Do you change colour?
VALENTINE	Give him leave, madam, he is a kind of chameleon.
TURIO	That hath more mind to feed on your blood than live in your air.
VALENTINE	You have said, sir.
TURIO	Ay, sir, and done too, for this time.
VALENTINE	I know it well, sir: you always end ere you begin.
SILVIA	A fine volley of words, gentlemen, and quickly shot off.
VALENTINE	'Tis indeed, madam, we thank the giver.
SILVIA	Who is that, servant?
VALENTINE	Yourself, sweet lady, for you gave the fire. Sir Turio borrows his wit from your ladyship's looks, and spends what he borrows kindly in your company.
TURIO	Sir, if you spend word for word with me, I shall make your wit bankrupt.
VALENTINE	I know it well, sir: you have an exchequer of words and, I think, no other treasure to give your followers, for it appears by their bare liveries that they live by your bare words.
SILVIA	No more, gentlemen, no more: here comes my father.

[*Enter Duke*]

DUKE	Now, daughter Silvia, you are hard beset.
	Sir Valentine, your father is in good health:
	What say you to a letter from your friends
	Of much good news?
VALENTINE	My lord, I will be thankful
	To any happy messenger from thence.

25 **live . . . air** live near you/listen to you speak/live off the same air you breathe (like a chameleon)   28 **done** finished/acted (as opposed to having **said**)   **this time** the moment (Turio suggests that in the future he may "do" more, i.e. fight Valentine)   29 **end . . . begin** stop before you've started (i.e. before actually dueling)   30 **volley** discharge (of weapons)   34 **the fire** i.e. the spark to set off the **volley**/ignite the guns   36 **kindly** naturally/lovingly   37 **spend** spend like money/waste   39 **exchequer** treasury   41 **bare liveries** shabby uniforms (worn by a gentleman's servants or dependents)   45 **hard beset** energetically besieged (by suitors)   50 **happy messenger** messenger bringing good news

DUKE   Know ye Don Antonio, your countryman?

VALENTINE   Ay, my good lord, I know the gentleman
    To be of worth and worthy estimation,
    And not without desert so well reputed.

55 DUKE   Hath he not a son?

VALENTINE   Ay, my good lord, a son that well deserves
    The honour and regard of such a father.

DUKE   You know him well?

VALENTINE   I knew him as myself, for from our infancy

60 We have conversed and spent our hours together,
    And though myself have been an idle truant,
    Omitting the sweet benefit of time
    To clothe mine age with angel-like perfection,
    Yet hath Sir Proteus — for that's his name —

65 Made use and fair advantage of his days:
    His years but young, but his experience old,
    His head unmellowed but his judgement ripe,
    And in a word — for far behind his worth
    Comes all the praises that I now bestow —

70 He is complete in feature and in mind,
    With all good grace to grace a gentleman.

DUKE   Beshrew me, sir, but if he make this good,
    He is as worthy for an empress' love,
    As meet to be an emperor's counsellor.

75 Well, sir, this gentleman is come to me,
    With commendation from great potentates,
    And here he means to spend his time awhile:
    I think 'tis no unwelcome news to you.

VALENTINE   Should I have wished a thing, it had been he.

80 DUKE   Welcome him then according to his worth.
    Silvia, I speak to you, and you, Sir Turio,

---

51 **countryman** man from the same country   53 **worth** wealth/rank/worthiness   **worthy estimation** deserving of respect   54 **without desert** undeservedly   62 **Omitting** disregarding   63 **age** present age/eventual old age   67 **unmellowed** young (with no gray hairs)   **ripe** mature   70 **complete** perfect   **feature** physical appearance   72 **make this good** lives up to this description   76 **potentates** powerful rulers

For Valentine, I need not cite him to it:
I will send him hither to you presently.   [*Exit*]

VALENTINE   This is the gentleman I told your ladyship

85   Had come along with me, but that his mistress
Did hold his eyes locked in her crystal looks.

SILVIA   Belike that now she hath enfranchised them
Upon some other pawn for fealty.

VALENTINE   Nay, sure, I think she holds them prisoners still.

90   SILVIA   Nay, then he should be blind, and being blind,
How could he see his way to seek out you?

VALENTINE   Why, lady, Love hath twenty pair of eyes.

TURIO   They say that Love hath not an eye at all.

VALENTINE   To see such lovers, Turio, as yourself:

95   Upon a homely object, Love can wink.

SILVIA   Have done, have done: here comes the gentleman.

                                    [*Turio may exit*]

[*Enter Proteus*]

VALENTINE   Welcome, dear Proteus! Mistress, I beseech you,
Confirm his welcome with some special favour.

SILVIA   His worth is warrant for his welcome hither,

100   If this be he you oft have wished to hear from.

VALENTINE   Mistress, it is: sweet lady, entertain him
To be my fellow-servant to your ladyship.

SILVIA   Too low a mistress for so high a servant.

PROTEUS   Not so, sweet lady: but too mean a servant

105   To have a look of such a worthy mistress.

VALENTINE   Leave off discourse of disability:
Sweet lady, entertain him for your servant.

PROTEUS   My duty will I boast of, nothing else.

SILVIA   And duty never yet did want his meed.

110   Servant, you are welcome to a worthless mistress.

---

82 cite urge   **85 Had come** would have come   **86 looks** gaze   **87 Belike that** perhaps
enfranchised . . . fealty freed his eyes in return for an alternative pledge of loyalty/freed them
in favor of another lover's pledge of loyalty   **93 Love . . . all** Cupid was blind   **95 homely**
plain/unattractive   **wink** shut its eyes   **99 warrant** guarantee   **101 entertain** receive
103 low humble/short   **high** dignified/superior/tall   **104 mean** unworthy   **106 Leave . . .
disability** stop this talk of inadequacy   **108 duty** i.e. a servant's duty   **109 want his meed**
lack its recompense

PROTEUS   I'll die on him that says so but yourself.

SILVIA   That you are welcome?

PROTEUS   That you are worthless.

[*Enter Turio, or a servant enters and whispers to Turio*]

TURIO   Madam, my lord your father would speak with you.

115 SILVIA   I wait upon his pleasure. Come, Sir Turio,
Go with me. Once more, new servant, welcome.
I'll leave you to confer of home affairs:
When you have done, we look to hear from you.

PROTEUS   We'll both attend upon your ladyship.

[*Exeunt Silvia and Turio*]

120 VALENTINE   Now, tell me: how do all from whence you came?

PROTEUS   Your friends are well and have them much
commended.

VALENTINE   And how do yours?

PROTEUS   I left them all in health.

VALENTINE   How does your lady? And how thrives your love?

125 PROTEUS   My tales of love were wont to weary you:
I know you joy not in a love discourse.

VALENTINE   Ay, Proteus, but that life is altered now.
I have done penance for contemning Love,
Whose high imperious thoughts have punished me
130 With bitter fasts, with penitential groans,
With nightly tears and daily heart-sore sighs:
For in revenge of my contempt of love,
Love hath chased sleep from my enthrallèd eyes,
And made them watchers of mine own heart's sorrow.
135 O gentle Proteus, Love's a mighty lord,
And hath so humbled me, as I confess,
There is no woe to his correction,
Nor to his service no such joy on earth.
Now no discourse, except it be of love:

---

111 **die** i.e. in a fight   **but** except for   121 **them much commended** conveyed their
hearty greetings   125 **were wont to** used to   128 **contemning** condemning, despising
129 **imperious** magisterial/commanding   130 **penitential** undergoing penance
133 **enthrallèd** enslaved   134 **watchers of** sleepless over/vigilant over   137 **no . . . correction**
no misery as bad as that which results from Love's punishment   138 **to** in comparison to

140　Now can I break my fast, dine, sup and sleep
　　Upon the very naked name of love.
PROTEUS　Enough: I read your fortune in your eye.
　　Was this the idol that you worship so?
VALENTINE　Even she; and is she not a heavenly saint?
145 PROTEUS　No, but she is an earthly paragon.
VALENTINE　Call her divine.
PROTEUS　I will not flatter her.
VALENTINE　O, flatter me, for love delights in praises.
PROTEUS　When I was sick, you gave me bitter pills,
150　And I must minister the like to you.
VALENTINE　Then speak the truth by her; if not divine,
　　Yet let her be a principality,
　　Sovereign to all the creatures on the earth.
PROTEUS　Except my mistress.
155 VALENTINE　Sweet, except not any,
　　Except thou wilt except against my love.
PROTEUS　Have I not reason to prefer mine own?
VALENTINE　And I will help thee to prefer her too:
　　She shall be dignified with this high honour,
160　To bear my lady's train, lest the base earth
　　Should from her vesture chance to steal a kiss,
　　And of so great a favour growing proud,
　　Disdain to root the summer-swelling flower
　　And make rough winter everlastingly.
165 PROTEUS　Why, Valentine, what braggardism is this?
VALENTINE　Pardon me, Proteus: all I can is nothing
　　To her whose worth makes other worthies nothing.
　　She is alone.
PROTEUS　Then let her alone.

141 very naked mere   143 this i.e. Silvia   144 Even she she indeed/exactly so   145 paragon
person of surpassing excellence   149 sick i.e. with love (for Julia)   bitter pills i.e. did not
indulge me, but administered unpleasant-tasting medicine   150 minister the like give you the
same treatment   151 by about   152 principality one of the nine orders of angels   155 Sweet
a term of friendly affection   156 Except unless   except against object to   158 prefer
promote, advance   161 from . . . kiss brush against her clothing   163 Disdain . . . flower
refuse to allow the flowers to take root in it   165 braggardism bragging arrogance   166 can
i.e. can say   167 To compared to   worthies things of value   168 alone unique

170   VALENTINE   Not for the world: why, man, she is mine own,
　　　　And I as rich in having such a jewel
　　　　As twenty seas, if all their sand were pearl,
　　　　The water nectar, and the rocks pure gold.
　　　　Forgive me that I do not dream on thee,
175　　Because thou see'st me dote upon my love.
　　　　My foolish rival, that her father likes —
　　　　Only for his possessions are so huge —
　　　　Is gone with her along, and I must after:
　　　　For love, thou know'st, is full of jealousy.
180   PROTEUS   But she loves you?
　　　　VALENTINE   Ay, and we are betrothed: nay, more, our marriage-
　　　　　　hour,
　　　　With all the cunning manner of our flight,
　　　　Determined of: how I must climb her window,
　　　　The ladder made of cords, and all the means
185　　Plotted and 'greed on for my happiness.
　　　　Good Proteus, go with me to my chamber,
　　　　In these affairs to aid me with thy counsel.
　　　　PROTEUS   Go on before: I shall inquire you forth.
　　　　I must unto the road, to disembark
190　　Some necessaries that I needs must use,
　　　　And then I'll presently attend you.
　　　　VALENTINE   Will you make haste?
　　　　PROTEUS   I will.　　　　　　　　　　　　*Exit* [*Valentine*]
　　　　Even as one heat another heat expels,
195　　Or as one nail by strength drives out another,
　　　　So the remembrance of my former love
　　　　Is by a newer object quite forgotten.
　　　　Is it mine eye or Valentine's praise?
　　　　Her true perfection or my false transgression

---

174 **dream on thee** pay you much attention   175 **dote upon** focus lovingly on/be infatuated with   177 **for** because   182 **With . . . flight** along with every detail of our ingenious escape plan   183 **Determined of** decided on   185 **'greed** agreed   188 **inquire you forth** seek you out   189 **disembark** unload (from the boat)   190 **necessaries** personal luggage   194 **expels** drives out (applying heat was thought to ease a burn)   196 **remembrance** memory   197 **object** sight   199 **false transgression** faithless sin/wrongful violation of loyalty

200 That makes me reasonless to reason thus?
 She is fair: and so is Julia that I love —
 That I did love, for now my love is thawed,
 Which, like a waxen image gainst a fire
 Bears no impression of the thing it was.
205 Methinks my zeal to Valentine is cold,
 And that I love him not as I was wont.
 O, but I love his lady too too much,
 And that's the reason I love him so little.
 How shall I dote on her with more advice,
210 That thus without advice begin to love her?
 'Tis but her picture I have yet beheld,
 And that hath dazzlèd my reason's light:
 But when I look on her perfections,
 There is no reason but I shall be blind.
215 If I can check my erring love, I will:
 If not, to compass her I'll use my skill.   *Exit*

Act 2 Scene 5

running scene 8

Enter Speed and Lance [separately. Lance with his dog, Crab]

SPEED Lance, by mine honesty, welcome to Padua.

LANCE Forswear not thyself, sweet youth, for I am not
 welcome. I reckon this always, that a man is never undone
 till he be hanged, nor never welcome to a place till some
5 certain shot be paid and the hostess say 'Welcome!'

---

200 reasonless without cause **to reason thus** justify myself/explore matters in this way
205 zeal devotion/loyalty **209 advice** reflection **210 without advice** unadvisedly
211 picture appearance **213 look** come to look (in the future) **perfections** exquisite inner
qualities **214 no reason but** no doubt that **215 check** restrain/reprimand **erring**
wandering/wrongful **216 compass** win/embrace **2.5** **1 Padua** most editors emend to
"Milan," assuming that Shakespeare forgot his location, but it is conceivable that Speed is
winding up the travel-weary and slow-witted Lance by naming the wrong city **2 Forswear**
swear falsely/perjure (Lance claims that he is not **welcome**, but may also imply cheekily that
Speed swears falsely because he does so on his **honesty**) **3 reckon** think/add up **undone**
ruined (puns on the notion of untying a **hanged** body) **5 shot** payment/tavern bill **hostess**
landlady of an inn

SPEED Come on, you madcap: I'll to the ale-house with you presently, where, for one shot of five pence, thou shalt have five thousand welcomes. But, sirrah, how did thy master part with Madam Julia?

10 LANCE Marry, after they closed in earnest, they parted very fairly in jest.

SPEED But shall she marry him?

LANCE No.

SPEED How then? Shall he marry her?

15 LANCE No, neither.

SPEED What, are they broken?

LANCE No, they are both as whole as a fish.

SPEED Why then, how stands the matter with them?

LANCE Marry, thus: when it stands well with him, it stands
20 well with her.

SPEED What an ass art thou! I understand thee not.

LANCE What a block art thou, that thou canst not! My staff understands me.

SPEED What thou say'st?

25 LANCE Ay, and what I do too: look thee, I'll but lean, and my staff under-stands me.

SPEED It stands under thee, indeed.

LANCE Why, stand-under and under-stand is all one.

SPEED But tell me true, will't be a match?

30 LANCE Ask my dog: if he say 'ay', it will. If he say 'no', it will. If he shake his tail and say nothing, it will.

SPEED The conclusion is, then, that it will.

LANCE Thou shalt never get such a secret from me but by a parable.

---

10 closed in earnest embraced/agreed in a serious manner (there may also be a glance at the sense of **earnest** as "financial pledge," thus contributing to the banter about money) **11 fairly** kindly/cordially **16 broken** fallen out (in the following line Lance plays on "in pieces")
17 as . . . fish proverbial (**whole** puns on "hole," which, along with **fish** was slang for "vagina")
18 stands the matter goes the business (**stands** puns on "to become erect" and **matter** on "sexual liaison"; Lance picks up on this in the following line) **22 block** blockhead
23 understands stands beneath/supports (puns on Speed's sense of "comprehend"; the staff may be used to suggest a penis) **34 parable** comparison/enigmatic speech

35 SPEED	'Tis well that I get it so. But Lance, how say'st thou that my master is become a notable lover?
LANCE	I never knew him otherwise.
SPEED	Than how?
LANCE	A notable lubber, as thou reportest him to be.
40 SPEED	Why, thou whoreson ass, thou mistak'st me.
LANCE	Why, fool, I meant not thee, I meant thy master.
SPEED	I tell thee, my master is become a hot lover.
LANCE	Why, I tell thee, I care not though he burn himself in love. If thou wilt, go with me to the alehouse: if not, thou
45	art an Hebrew, a Jew, and not worth the name of a Christian.
SPEED	Why?
LANCE	Because thou hast not so much charity in thee as to go to the ale with a Christian. Wilt thou go?
SPEED	At thy service. *Exeunt*

Act 2 Scene 6

running scene 9

Enter Proteus alone

PROTEUS	To leave my Julia, shall I be forsworn?
	To love fair Silvia, shall I be forsworn?
	To wrong my friend, I shall be much forsworn.
	And ev'n that power which gave me first my oath
5	Provokes me to this threefold perjury.
	Love bade me swear, and Love bids me forswear;
	O sweet-suggesting Love, if thou hast sinned,
	Teach me, thy tempted subject, to excuse it.
	At first I did adore a twinkling star,

---

35 how say'st thou what do you say to the suggestion   **36 notable** noticeable/notorious
39 lubber clumsy lout   **40 whoreson** bastard (whore's son)   **thou mistak'st me** you
misunderstand me (Lance interprets "you mistake me, Speed, for my **master**, Valentine")
48 ale alehouse/country festival (possibly a church festival, which a Jew would not attend;
alternatively Lance may be associating Jewishness with a lack of Christian **charity**)
2.6   4 power . . . oath love, which made me swear fidelity to Julia   **7 sweet-suggesting**
sweetly tempting/seductive   **if . . . it** if you have ever sinned/if you have sinned by making me
false (to Julia), teach me how to justify it

10   But now I worship a celestial sun.
Unheedful vows may heedfully be broken,
And he wants wit that wants resolvèd will
To learn his wit t'exchange the bad for better.
Fie, fie, unreverend tongue, to call her bad,
15   Whose sovereignty so oft thou hast preferred
With twenty thousand soul-confirming oaths.
I cannot leave to love, and yet I do:
But there I leave to love where I should love.
Julia I lose, and Valentine I lose:
20   If I keep them, I needs must lose myself.
If I lose them, thus find I by their loss:
For Valentine, myself, for Julia, Silvia.
I to myself am dearer than a friend,
For love is still most precious in itself,
25   And Silvia — witness heaven that made her fair—
Shows Julia but a swarthy Ethiope.
I will forget that Julia is alive,
Remembering that my love to her is dead.
And Valentine I'll hold an enemy,
30   Aiming at Silvia as a sweeter friend.
I cannot now prove constant to myself,
Without some treachery used to Valentine.
This night he meaneth with a corded ladder
To climb celestial Silvia's chamber-window,
35   Myself in counsel his competitor.
Now presently I'll give her father notice
Of their disguising and pretended flight,
Who, all enraged, will banish Valentine,

---

11 Unheedful thoughtless   **heedfully** carefully/conscientiously   **12 wants wit** lacks intelligence   **13 learn** teach   **14 unreverend** irreverent, impudent   **her** i.e. Julia   **15 preferred** urged   **16 soul-confirming** soul-strengthening (Proteus has sworn by his soul)   **17 leave** cease   **21 thus find I** so I find myself   **22 For** in exchange for   **25 fair** beautiful/pale complexioned   **26 Shows Julia** reveals, shows up Julia to be   **swarthy Ethiope** dark-complexioned Ethiopian (considered unattractive)   **29 hold** consider   **31 constant** faithful, true   **33 corded** rope   **35 in counsel** being in his confidence   **competitor** associate/rival   **37 disguising . . . flight** deceptive intended escape

For Turio he intends shall wed his daughter.

40 But Valentine being gone, I'll quickly cross,

By some sly trick, blunt Turio's dull proceeding.

Love, lend me wings to make my purpose swift,

As thou hast lent me wit to plot this drift.   *Exit*

Act 2 Scene 7   *running scene 10*

Enter Julia and Lucetta

JULIA   Counsel, Lucetta: gentle girl, assist me,

And ev'n in kind love, I do conjure thee,

Who art the table wherein all my thoughts

Are visibly charactered and engraved,

5 To lesson me and tell me some good mean

How with my honour I may undertake

A journey to my loving Proteus.

LUCETTA   Alas, the way is wearisome and long.

JULIA   A true-devoted pilgrim is not weary

10 To measure kingdoms with his feeble steps:

Much less shall she that hath Love's wings to fly,

And when the flight is made to one so dear,

Of such divine perfection as Sir Proteus.

LUCETTA   Better forbear till Proteus make return.

15 JULIA   O, know'st thou not his looks are my soul's food?

Pity the dearth that I have pined in,

By longing for that food so long a time.

Didst thou but know the inly touch of love,

Thou wouldst as soon go kindle fire with snow

20 As seek to quench the fire of love with words.

LUCETTA   I do not seek to quench your love's hot fire,

But qualify the fire's extreme rage,

Lest it should burn above the bounds of reason.

---

40 **cross** thwart   41 **blunt** stupid   42 **lend** give   43 **drift** scheme   **2.7 *Location: Verona***
2 **conjure** entreat   3 **table** writing tablet, notebook   4 **charactered** written   5 **lesson** teach
mean method   10 **measure** travel over   14 **forbear** have patience/desist   16 **dearth** famine
18 **inly** inward   22 **qualify** moderate

JULIA   The more thou damm'st it up, the more it burns.
25   The current that with gentle murmur glides,
          Thou know'st, being stopped, impatiently doth rage:
          But when his fair course is not hinderèd,
          He makes sweet music with th'enamelled stones,
          Giving a gentle kiss to every sedge
30   He overtaketh in his pilgrimage,
          And so by many winding nooks he strays
          With willing sport to the wild ocean.
          Then let me go, and hinder not my course:
          I'll be as patient as a gentle stream,
35   And make a pastime of each weary step,
          Till the last step have brought me to my love,
          And there I'll rest, as after much turmoil
          A blessèd soul doth in Elysium.

LUCETTA   But in what habit will you go along?
40   JULIA   Not like a woman, for I would prevent
          The loose encounters of lascivious men:
          Gentle Lucetta, fit me with such weeds
          As may beseem some well-reputed page.

LUCETTA   Why then, your ladyship must cut your hair.
45   JULIA   No, girl, I'll knit it up in silken strings
          With twenty odd-conceited true-love knots.
          To be fantastic may become a youth
          Of greater time than I shall show to be.

LUCETTA   What fashion, madam, shall I make your breeches?
50   JULIA   That fits as well as 'Tell me, good my lord,
          What compass will you wear your farthingale?'
          Why, ev'n what fashion thou best likes, Lucetta.

LUCETTA   You must needs have them with a codpiece, madam.

---

25 current i.e. in water   **28 makes . . . stones** creates a pleasing sound as it babbles over the
smooth stones   **29 sedge** rush-like plant   **32 sport** entertaining activity   **wild** open/
untamed   **38 Elysium** heaven   **39 habit** clothing   **40 for . . . men** as I wish to avoid the
improper advances made by lewd men   **42 weeds** garments   **43 beseem** be appropriate for
45 knit tie, knot   **46 odd-conceited** elaborately devised   **47 fantastic** imaginative, fanciful
48 time age   **51 compass** circumference   **farthingale** hooped petticoat   **53 codpiece**
conspicuous attachment sewn onto the front of breeches (also implies the penis)

| | JULIA | Out, out, Lucetta! That will be ill-favoured. |

55   LUCETTA   A round hose, madam, now's not worth a pin
    Unless you have a codpiece to stick pins on.

JULIA   Lucetta, as thou lov'st me, let me have
    What thou think'st meet and is most mannerly.
    But tell me, wench, how will the world repute me
60   For undertaking so unstaid a journey?
    I fear me it will make me scandalized.

LUCETTA   If you think so, then stay at home and go not.

JULIA   Nay, that I will not.

LUCETTA   Then never dream on infamy, but go.
65   If Proteus like your journey when you come,
    No matter who's displeased when you are gone:
    I fear me he will scarce be pleased withal.

JULIA   That is the least, Lucetta, of my fear:
    A thousand oaths, an ocean of his tears,
70   And instances of infinite of love
    Warrant me welcome to my Proteus.

LUCETTA   All these are servants to deceitful men.

JULIA   Base men, that use them to so base effect.
    But truer stars did govern Proteus' birth:
75   His words are bonds, his oaths are oracles,
    His love sincere, his thoughts immaculate,
    His tears pure messengers sent from his heart,
    His heart, as far from fraud as heaven from earth.

LUCETTA   Pray heav'n he prove so when you come to him.

80   JULIA   Now, as thou lov'st me, do him not that wrong
    To bear a hard opinion of his truth:
    Only deserve my love by loving him,
    And presently go with me to my chamber

---

54 ill-favoured unsightly   **55 round hose** breeches with close-fitting legs that gave a padded appearance to the upper area; usually adorned with a prominent codpiece   **not . . . pin** not worth anything/not worthy of a penis   **56 stick pins on** some codpieces were decorated with pins   **58 mannerly** appropriate (puns on "man")   **60 unstaid** immodest   **61 scandalized** disgraced   **64 dream on infamy** worry about getting a bad reputation   **67 withal** with it   **70 instances** evidence   **infinite** infinity   **71 Warrant . . . Proteus** guarantee that Proteus will welcome my arrival   **75 bonds** binding promises   **oracles** guaranteed truth-tellers   **76 immaculate** pure   **81 hard** poor   **truth** sincerity/fidelity

To take a note of what I stand in need of,
85 To furnish me upon my longing journey.
All that is mine I leave at thy dispose,
My goods, my lands, my reputation:
Only, in lieu thereof, dispatch me hence.
Come, answer not, but to it presently.
90 I am impatient of my tarriance.   *Exeunt*

Act 3 Scene 1   *running scene 11*

Enter Duke, Turio [and] Proteus

DUKE   Sir Turio, give us leave, I pray, awhile:
We have some secrets to confer about.   [*Exit Turio*]
Now, tell me, Proteus, what's your will with me?
PROTEUS   My gracious lord, that which I would discover
5   The law of friendship bids me to conceal,
But when I call to mind your gracious favours
Done to me — undeserving as I am —
My duty pricks me on to utter that
Which else no worldly good should draw from me.
10   Know, worthy prince, Sir Valentine my friend
This night intends to steal away your daughter:
Myself am one made privy to the plot.
I know you have determined to bestow her
On Turio, whom your gentle daughter hates,
15   ·And should she thus be stol'n away from you,
It would be much vexation to your age.
Thus, for my duty's sake, I rather chose
To cross my friend in his intended drift,
Than, by concealing it, heap on your head
20   A pack of sorrows which would press you down,
Being unprevented, to your timeless grave.

---

85 **furnish** maintain/equip   **longing journey** journey undertaken as a result of longing   **86 at
thy dispose** under your control   **88 in lieu thereof** in exchange for which   **90 tarriance** delay
3.1 Location: Milan   **1 give us leave** leave us (polite)   **8 pricks** spurs   **12 privy to** aware
of/entrusted with   **16 vexation** anger/distress   **21 timeless** premature

DUKE   Proteus, I thank thee for thine honest care,
            Which to requite, command me while I live.
            This love of theirs myself have often seen,
25   Haply when they have judged me fast asleep,
            And oftentimes have purposed to forbid
            Sir Valentine her company and my court.
            But fearing lest my jealous aim might err
            And so unworthily disgrace the man —
30   A rashness that I ever yet have shunned —
            I gave him gentle looks, thereby to find
            That which thyself hast now disclosed to me.
            And that thou mayst perceive my fear of this,
            Knowing that tender youth is soon suggested,
35   I nightly lodge her in an upper tower,
            The key whereof myself have ever kept:
            And thence she cannot be conveyed away.

PROTEUS   Know, noble lord, they have devised a mean
            How he her chamber-window will ascend,
40   And with a corded ladder fetch her down:
            For which, the youthful lover now is gone,
            And this way comes he with it presently,
            Where, if it please you, you may intercept him.
            But, good my lord, do it so cunningly
45   That my discovery be not aimed at:
            For love of you, not hate unto my friend,
            Hath made me publisher of this pretence.

DUKE   Upon mine honour, he shall never know
            That I had any light from thee of this.

50   PROTEUS   Adieu, my lord: Sir Valentine is coming.

                                                      [*Exit Proteus*]

            [*Enter Valentine*]

---

23 requite repay   **command me** ask any favor of me   **26 purposed** intended   **28 jealous aim**
suspicious guess   **31 gentle** kind/friendly/courteous   **thereby . . . me** in order to try
and discover the information you have just revealed to me   **34 suggested** tempted
45 discovery . . . at revelation that Proteus exposed Valentine's secret is not suspected
47 publisher revealer   **pretence** intention   **49 light** enlightenment, indication

	DUKE	Sir Valentine, whither away so fast?
	VALENTINE	Please it your grace, there is a messenger
		That stays to bear my letters to my friends,
		And I am going to deliver them.
55	DUKE	Be they of much import?
	VALENTINE	The tenor of them doth but signify
		My health and happy being at your court.
	DUKE	Nay then, no matter. Stay with me awhile:
		I am to break with thee of some affairs
60		That touch me near, wherein thou must be secret.
		'Tis not unknown to thee that I have sought
		To match my friend Sir Turio to my daughter.
	VALENTINE	I know it well, my lord, and sure the match
		Were rich and honourable: besides, the gentleman
65		Is full of virtue, bounty, worth and qualities
		Beseeming such a wife as your fair daughter.
		Cannot your grace win her to fancy him?
	DUKE	No, trust me, she is peevish, sullen, froward,
		Proud, disobedient, stubborn, lacking duty,
70		Neither regarding that she is my child
		Nor fearing me as if I were her father.
		And, may I say to thee, this pride of hers,
		Upon advice, hath drawn my love from her,
		And, where I thought the remnant of mine age
75		Should have been cherished by her child-like duty,
		I now am full resolved to take a wife
		And turn her out to who will take her in:
		Then let her beauty be her wedding-dower,
		For me and my possessions she esteems not.
80	VALENTINE	What would your grace have me to do in this?
	DUKE	There is a lady in Verona here

51 **whither away** where are you going   **56 tenor** content   **59 am to break** want to broach
60 touch me near affect me significantly, are close to my heart   **65 bounty** generosity
66 Beseeming befitting   **68 peevish** headstrong   **froward** obstinate   **70 regarding**
considering/respecting   **71 as . . . were** as she should do toward   **73 advice** reflection
74 remnant . . . age remainder of my days   **77 who** whoever   **78 wedding-dower** dowry
79 esteems values

Whom I affect: but she is nice and coy,
And nought esteems my agèd eloquence.
Now therefore would I have thee to my tutor —
85 For long agone I have forgot to court,
Besides, the fashion of the time is changed —
How and which way I may bestow myself
To be regarded in her sun-bright eye.
VALENTINE   Win her with gifts, if she respect not words:
90 Dumb jewels often in their silent kind
More than quick words do move a woman's mind.
DUKE   But she did scorn a present that I sent her.
VALENTINE   A woman sometime scorns what best contents her.
Send her another: never give her o'er,
95 For scorn at first makes after-love the more.
If she do frown, 'tis not in hate of you,
But rather to beget more love in you.
If she do chide, 'tis not to have you gone,
Forwhy, the fools are mad, if left alone.
100 Take no repulse, whatever she doth say,
For 'get you gone', she doth not mean 'away!'
Flatter and praise, commend, extol their graces:
Though ne'er so black, say they have angels' faces.
That man that hath a tongue, I say is no man
105 If with his tongue he cannot win a woman.
DUKE   But she I mean is promised by her friends
Unto a youthful gentleman of worth,
And kept severely from resort of men,
That no man hath access by day to her.
110 VALENTINE   Why then I would resort to her by night.

82 **affect** love/favor **nice** reluctant/temperamental 83 **nought . . . eloquence** does not care for the love-talk of an old man 85 **agone** ago **forgot to court** forgotten how to woo 87 **bestow myself** behave 88 **regarded** well regarded 90 **kind** nature 91 **quick** lively 94 **her o'er** up on her 95 **after-love the more** later love greater 97 **beget** produce 99 **Forwhy** because 101 **For** by 102 **commend** praise **extol their graces** elaborate on their virtues 103 **Though . . . black** however dark-complexioned/unattractive they be 105 **with his tongue** through talking/flattery (plays on the idea of oral sex) 106 **friends** family 109 **That** so that

DUKE   Ay, but the doors be locked and keys kept safe,
              That no man hath recourse to her by night.
VALENTINE   What lets but one may enter at her window?
DUKE   Her chamber is aloft, far from the ground,
115   And built so shelving that one cannot climb it
              Without apparent hazard of his life.
VALENTINE   Why then, a ladder quaintly made of cords
              To cast up, with a pair of anchoring hooks,
              Would serve to scale another Hero's tower,
120   So bold Leander would adventure it.
DUKE   Now, as thou art a gentleman of blood,
              Advise me where I may have such a ladder.
VALENTINE   When would you use it? Pray, sir, tell me that.
DUKE   This very night; for Love is like a child
125   That longs for everything that he can come by.
VALENTINE   By seven o'clock I'll get you such a ladder.
DUKE   But, hark thee: I will go to her alone.
              How shall I best convey the ladder thither?
VALENTINE   It will be light, my lord, that you may bear it
130   Under a cloak that is of any length.
DUKE   A cloak as long as thine will serve the turn?
VALENTINE   Ay, my good lord.
DUKE   Then let me see thy cloak:
              I'll get me one of such another length.
135   VALENTINE   Why, any cloak will serve the turn, my lord.
DUKE   How shall I fashion me to wear a cloak?
              I pray thee, let me feel thy cloak upon me.   *Takes Valentine's cloak*
              What letter is this same? What's here? 'To Silvia'!   *and discovers a*
              And here an engine fit for my proceeding.   *letter and a rope ladder*
140   I'll be so bold to break the seal for once.   *concealed under it*

---

113 lets prevents   **115 shelving** projecting   **117 quaintly** skillfully   **118 anchoring hooks**
heavy hooks attached to the rope ladder as a means of securing it to the window   **119 Hero's
tower** in classical myth, Leander was guided to Hero by a light in her tower   **120 So** provided
121 blood rank/good family   **130 of any length** reasonably long   **131 serve the turn** fit the
purpose   **134 such another** the same   **136 fashion me** adapt myself   **138 this same** this one
here   **139 engine . . . proceeding** device (the ladder) suitable for the very scheme I have been
planning

'My thoughts do harbour with my Silvia nightly,   *Reads*
And slaves they are to me that send them flying.
O, could their master come and go as lightly,
Himself would lodge where, senseless, they are lying.
145 My herald thoughts in thy pure bosom rest them,
While I, their king, that thither them importune,
Do curse the grace that with such grace hath blessed them,
Because myself do want my servants' fortune.
I curse myself, for they are sent by me,
150 That they should harbour where their lord should be.'
What's here?
'Silvia, this night I will enfranchise thee.'
'Tis so: and here's the ladder for the purpose.
Why, Phaeton — for thou art Merops' son —
155 Wilt thou aspire to guide the heavenly car,
And with thy daring folly burn the world?
Wilt thou reach stars because they shine on thee?
Go, base intruder, overweening slave,
Bestow thy fawning smiles on equal mates,
160 And think my patience, more than thy desert,
Is privilege for thy departure hence.
Thank me for this more than for all the favours
Which, all too much, I have bestowed on thee.
But if thou linger in my territories
165 Longer than swiftest expedition
Will give thee time to leave our royal court,
By heaven, my wrath shall far exceed the love
I ever bore my daughter or thyself.

---

141 **harbour** lodge/take refuge   143 **lightly** freely, easily   144 **Himself** i.e. Valentine
senseless unconscious   **lying** reposing/dwelling   145 **herald** messenger   **them** themselves
146 **thither them importune** urge them to go there   147 **grace . . . grace** good fortune that
with such honor   148 **want** lack   **servants'** i.e. thoughts'   152 **enfranchise** liberate
154 **Phaeton . . . son** in Greek mythology Phaeton was the son of the sun god Helios and
Clymene (wife of **Merops**); he drove Helios' sun chariot (**heavenly car**), but could not control it,
burned part of the earth and was killed with a thunderbolt hurled by Zeus   158 **overweening**
slave arrogant rogue   159 **equal mates** women of your own worth/social status
160 **And . . . hence** know that it is my patience, rather than any merit of your own that is
responsible for permitting you to leave   165 **expedition** departure

Be gone! I will not hear thy vain excuse,
170 But as thou lov'st thy life, make speed from hence.   [*Exit*]
VALENTINE   And why not death, rather than living torment?
To die is to be banished from myself,
And Silvia is myself: banished from her
Is self from self. A deadly banishment:
175 What light is light, if Silvia be not seen?
What joy is joy, if Silvia be not by?
Unless it be to think that she is by
And feed upon the shadow of perfection.
Except I be by Silvia in the night,
180 There is no music in the nightingale.
Unless I look on Silvia in the day,
There is no day for me to look upon.
She is my essence, and I leave to be
If I be not by her fair influence
185 Fostered, illumined, cherished, kept alive.
I fly not death, to fly his deadly doom:
Tarry I here, I but attend on death,
But fly I hence, I fly away from life.
[*Enter Proteus and Lance*]
PROTEUS   Run, boy, run, run, and seek him out.
190 LANCE   So-ho, so-ho!
PROTEUS   What see'st thou?
LANCE   Him we go to find: there's not a hair on's head but
'tis a Valentine.
PROTEUS   Valentine?
195 VALENTINE   No.
PROTEUS   Who then? His spirit?
VALENTINE   Neither.
PROTEUS   What then?

---

176 **by** nearby   178 **shadow** image   179 **Except** unless   183 **leave to be** cease to exist
184 **influence** power/substance thought to emanate from stars that influenced human fate
185 **Fostered** nurtured   **illumined** lit up   186 **I . . . doom** I am not really escaping death in
fleeing the duke's sentence (**doom**)   187 **attend on** wait for/serve   190 **So-ho** a hunting cry
192 **hair** puns on "hare"   193 **a Valentine** a true lover/token of love (Valentine is a lover right
down to his very hairs)   196 **spirit** ghost

	VALENTINE	Nothing.
200	LANCE	Can nothing speak? Master, shall I strike?
	PROTEUS	Who wouldst thou strike?
	LANCE	Nothing.
	PROTEUS	Villain, forbear.
	LANCE	Why, sir, I'll strike nothing. I pray you—
205	PROTEUS	Sirrah, I say forbear. Friend Valentine, a word.
	VALENTINE	My ears are stopped and cannot hear good news,

VALENTINE My ears are stopped and cannot hear good news,
   So much of bad already hath possessed them.

PROTEUS Then in dumb silence will I bury mine,
   For they are harsh, untuneable and bad.

210 VALENTINE Is Silvia dead?

PROTEUS No, Valentine.

VALENTINE No Valentine indeed, for sacred Silvia.
   Hath she forsworn me?

PROTEUS No, Valentine.

215 VALENTINE No Valentine, if Silvia have forsworn me.
   What is your news?

LANCE Sir, there is a proclamation that you are vanished.

PROTEUS That thou art banished — O, that's the news —
   From hence, from Silvia, and from me thy friend.

220 VALENTINE O, I have fed upon this woe already,
   And now excess of it will make me surfeit.
   Doth Silvia know that I am banishèd?

PROTEUS Ay, ay: and she hath offered to the doom —
   Which unreversed stands in effectual force —

225 A sea of melting pearl, which some call tears:
Those at her father's churlish feet she tendered,
With them, upon her knees, her humble self,
Wringing her hands, whose whiteness so became them

---

203 **Villain** rogue   204 **I'll strike nothing** I won't hit anything/if I hit a spirit I will be striking nothing as it has no body   206 **stopped** blocked   208 **mine** i.e. my news   212 **No Valentine** no longer able to be a lover/no longer myself (as existence was dependent on Silvia's presence) 213 **forsworn** rejected   217 **vanished** malapropism for "banished"   221 **surfeit** be ill from overeating   223 **doom . . . force** the sentence of banishment which, as long as it is not reversed, stands in full force   226 **tendered** made an offering of   228 **became** suited

As if but now they waxèd pale for woe.
230 But neither bended knees, pure hands held up,
Sad sighs, deep groans, nor silver-shedding tears
Could penetrate her uncompassionate sire;
But Valentine, if he be ta'en, must die.
Besides, her intercession chafed him so,
235 When she for thy repeal was suppliant,
That to close prison he commanded her,
With many bitter threats of biding there.

VALENTINE   No more, unless the next word that thou speak'st
Have some malignant power upon my life:
240 If so, I pray thee breathe it in mine ear,
As ending anthem of my endless dolour.

PROTEUS   Cease to lament for that thou canst not help,
And study help for that which thou lament'st:
Time is the nurse and breeder of all good.
245 Here if thou stay, thou canst not see thy love:
Besides, thy staying will abridge thy life.
Hope is a lover's staff: walk hence with that
And manage it against despairing thoughts.
Thy letters may be here, though thou art hence,
250 Which, being writ to me, shall be delivered
Even in the milk-white bosom of thy love.
The time now serves not to expostulate:
Come, I'll convey thee through the city-gate,
And ere I part with thee, confer at large
255 Of all that may concern thy love-affairs.
As thou lov'st Silvia, though not for thyself,
Regard thy danger, and along with me.

---

229 **waxèd** grew   232 **sire** father   234 **intercession** prayer on someone else's behalf   **chafed**
enraged   235 **thy repeal** the reversal of your sentence/your return   **suppliant** petitioner
236 **close** secure/secluded   237 **biding** (her) remaining   239 **malignant** evil/harmful/
infectious   241 **As . . . dolour** so that it might be a funeral hymn to my infinite sorrow
243 **study** think about   246 **abridge** shorten   248 **manage** handle, wield   251 **thy love**
i.e. Silvia   252 **expostulate** discuss/expound   254 **confer at large** discuss in full
256 **though . . . thyself** even if not for your own sake   257 **Regard** pay heed to

VALENTINE   I pray thee, Lance, an if thou see'st my boy,
                    Bid him make haste and meet me at the North-gate.

260 PROTEUS   Go, sirrah, find him out. Come, Valentine.

VALENTINE   O, my dear Silvia! Hapless Valentine!

                    [*Exeunt Valentine and Proteus*]

LANCE   I am but a fool, look you, and yet I have the wit to
                    think my master is a kind of a knave: but that's all one, if he
                    be but one knave. He lives not now that knows me to be in
265   love, yet I am in love, but a team of horse shall not pluck that
                    from me, nor who 'tis I love: and yet 'tis a woman, but what
                    woman, I will not tell myself: and yet 'tis a milkmaid, yet
                    'tis not a maid, for she hath had gossips: yet 'tis a maid, for
                    she is her master's maid, and serves for wages. She hath
270   more qualities than a water-spaniel, which is much in a
                    bare Christian. Here is the cate-log of her condition.   *Pulls out*
                    '*Imprimis*: She can fetch and carry.' Why, a horse can   *a paper*
                    do no more; nay, a horse cannot fetch, but only carry,
                    therefore is she better than a jade. '*Item*: She can milk.' Look
275   you, a sweet virtue in a maid with clean hands.

[*Enter Speed*]

SPEED   How now, Signior Lance? What news with your
                    mastership?

LANCE   With my master's ship? Why, it is at sea.

SPEED   Well, your old vice still: mistake the word. What
280   news, then, in your paper?

LANCE   The blackest news that ever thou heard'st.

SPEED   Why, man? How black?

---

258 **my boy** i.e. Speed   263 **all . . . knave** doesn't matter as long as he is a knave in one thing
only   264 **He . . . that** not a man alive   265 **horse** horses   268 **maid** virgin   **gossips**
godparents (i.e. she has had a child)   **maid** servant   269 **serves** provides domestic
service/has sex   270 **qualities** accomplishments   **water-spaniel** submissive dog   271 **bare**
mere/naked (i.e. not hairy like a dog)   **cate-log . . . condition** catalogue (list) of her attributes
272 *Imprimis* "in the first place" (Latin)   273 **fetch** respond to an instruction to fetch
something   274 **jade** worthless old horse/loose woman   *Item* Latin term for "next" (in a list)
milk milk a cow/drain one of money/suckle a baby/cause ejaculation (**clean hands** may
continue the idea of masturbation)   279 **vice** bad habit/comic character in morality plays
known for his puns

LANCE	Why, as black as ink.
SPEED	Let me read them.
285 LANCE	Fie on thee, jolt-head, thou canst not read.
SPEED	Thou liest: I can.
LANCE	I will try thee. Tell me this: who begot thee?
SPEED	Marry, the son of my grandfather.
LANCE	O illiterate loiterer! It was the son of thy
290	grandmother: this proves that thou canst not read.
SPEED	Come, fool, come: try me in thy paper.
LANCE	There: and Saint Nicholas be thy *Gives him the paper*
	speed.
SPEED	'*Imprimis*: She can milk.' *Reads*
LANCE	Ay, that she can.
295 SPEED	'*Item*: She brews good ale.'
LANCE	And thereof comes the proverb 'Blessing of your
	heart, you brew good ale.'
SPEED	'*Item*: She can sew.'
LANCE	That's as much as to say 'Can she so?'
300 SPEED	'*Item*: She can knit.'
LANCE	What need a man care for a stock with a wench,
	when she can knit him a stock?
SPEED	'*Item*: She can wash and scour.'
LANCE	A special virtue, for then she need not be washed
305	and scoured.
SPEED	'*Item:* She can spin.'
LANCE	Then may I set the world on wheels, when she can
	spin for her living.
SPEED	'*Item:* She hath many nameless virtues.'
310 LANCE	That's as much as to say 'bastard virtues' that
	indeed know not their fathers, and therefore have no names.

---

285 jolt-head blockhead   **287 try** test   **begot** conceived   **291 in** on   **292 Saint Nicholas** patron saint of scholars   **speed** protector (puns on Speed's name)   **298 sew** stitch (Lance interprets "sow seed" and is therefore surprised that a woman can do so)   **301 stock** dowry   **302 knit . . . stock** knit him a stocking/conceive stupid offspring for him   **304 washed and scoured** cleaned and scrubbed/beaten   **306 spin** spin wool/have sex   **307 set . . . wheels** have an easy life (**wheels** plays on "spinning-wheels")   **309 nameless virtues** inexpressible qualities   **310 bastard virtues** illegitimate children

SPEED	Here follow her vices.
LANCE	Close at the heels of her virtues.
SPEED	'Item: She is not to be kissed fasting in respect of her
315	breath.'
LANCE	Well, that fault may be mended with a breakfast.
	Read on.
SPEED	'Item: She hath a sweet mouth.'
LANCE	That makes amends for her sour breath.
320 SPEED	'Item: She doth talk in her sleep.'
LANCE	It's no matter for that, so she sleep not in her talk.
SPEED	'Item: She is slow in words.'
LANCE	O villain, that set this down among her vices! To be
	slow in words is a woman's only virtue: I pray thee out
325	with't, and place it for her chief virtue.
SPEED	'Item: She is proud.'
LANCE	Out with that too: it was Eve's legacy, and cannot be
	ta'en from her.
SPEED	'Item: She hath no teeth.'
330 LANCE	I care not for that neither, because I love crusts.
SPEED	'Item: She is curst.'
LANCE	Well, the best is, she hath no teeth to bite.
SPEED	'Item: She will often praise her liquor.'
LANCE	If her liquor be good, she shall: if she will not, I will,
335	for good things should be praised.
SPEED	'Item: She is too liberal.'
LANCE	Of her tongue she cannot, for that's writ down she
	is slow of: of her purse she shall not, for that I'll keep shut.
	Now, of another thing she may, and that cannot I help. Well,
340	proceed.

---

314 in respect of because of   **318 sweet mouth** sweet tooth/lecherous mouth   **321 sleep**
puns on "slip" (to commit an error/lapse sexually)   **326 proud** haughty/high-spirited/
lecherous   **327 Eve's legacy** the result of Eve's greedy desire in the Garden of Eden
329 no teeth possibly a result of having a **sweet mouth**, though teeth could also fall out after
treatment for syphilis   **331 curst** bad-tempered (plays on **crust**)   **333 praise** taste (in the
following line Lance has understood "speak highly of")   **336 liberal** unrestrained in her
manner/free with her sexual favors   **337 cannot** cannot be   **339 another thing** i.e. her vagina
(plays on **purse** which had the same slang meaning)

SPEED   '*Item:* She hath more hair than wit, and more faults
             than hairs, and more wealth than faults.'

LANCE   Stop there: I'll have her. She was mine and not
             mine, twice or thrice in that last article. Rehearse that once
345   more.

SPEED   '*Item:* She hath more hair than wit'—

LANCE   More hair than wit? It may be I'll prove it. The
             cover of the salt hides the salt, and therefore it is more than
             the salt; the hair that covers the wit is more than the wit, for
350   the greater hides the less. What's next?

SPEED   'And more faults than hairs'—

LANCE   That's monstrous: O, that that were out!

SPEED   'And more wealth than faults.'

LANCE   Why, that word makes the faults gracious. Well, I'll
355   have her: and if it be a match, as nothing is impossible—

SPEED   What then?

LANCE   Why, then will I tell thee — that thy master stays for
             thee at the North-gate.

SPEED   For me?

360   LANCE   For thee? Ay, who art thou? He hath stayed for a
             better man than thee.

SPEED   And must I go to him?

LANCE   Thou must run to him, for thou hast stayed so long
             that going will scarce serve the turn.

365   SPEED   Why didst not tell me sooner? Pox of' your love
             letters!   [*Exit*]

LANCE   Now will he be swinged for reading my letter; an
             unmannerly slave, that will thrust himself into secrets. I'll
             after, to rejoice in the boy's correction.   *Exit*

---

344 Rehearse repeat   **347 prove** i.e. with a verbal demonstration of logic   **348 more than**
greater than in that it entirely conceals the salt   **cover . . . salt** lid of a large salt cellar (**salt**
may pun on both "wit" and "lechery")   **352 monstrous** outrageous/unnatural   **out**
wrong/not on the list   **354 gracious** acceptable   **365 Pox of** a plague on   **367 swinged**
beaten   **368 unmannerly** ill-mannered   **I'll . . . correction** I'll follow so that I can enjoy seeing
his punishment (for being late)

Act 3 Scene 2

Enter Duke [and] Turio

DUKE	Sir Turio, fear not but that she will love you,
	Now Valentine is banished from her sight.
TURIO	Since his exile she hath despised me most,
	Forsworn my company and railed at me,
5		That I am desperate of obtaining her.
DUKE	This weak impress of love is as a figure
	Trenchèd in ice, which with an hour's heat
	Dissolves to water and doth lose his form.
	A little time will melt her frozen thoughts
10 | | And worthless Valentine shall be forgot. |

[Enter Proteus]

	How now, Sir Proteus, is your countryman,
	According to our proclamation, gone?
PROTEUS	Gone, my good lord.
DUKE	My daughter takes his going grievously?
15	PROTEUS	A little time, my lord, will kill that grief.
DUKE	So I believe, but Turio thinks not so.
	Proteus, the good conceit I hold of thee —
	For thou hast shown some sign of good desert—
	Makes me the better to confer with thee.
20	PROTEUS	Longer than I prove loyal to your grace
	Let me not live to look upon your grace.
DUKE	Thou know'st how willingly I would effect
	The match between Sir Turio and my daughter?
PROTEUS	I do, my lord.
25	DUKE	And also, I think, thou art not ignorant
	How she opposes her against my will?
PROTEUS	She did, my lord, when Valentine was here.

3.2   4 railed ranted abusively   **5 That** so that   **6 impress** impression, imprint   **figure** shape
7 Trenchèd cut, engraved   **14 grievously** sorrowfully   **17 conceit** opinion   **18 desert** worth,
deserving   **19 the better** more inclined   **22 effect** bring about

DUKE   Ay, and perversely she persevers so.
            What might we do to make the girl forget
30   The love of Valentine, and love Sir Turio?
PROTEUS   The best way is to slander Valentine
            With falsehood, cowardice and poor descent:
            Three things that women highly hold in hate.
DUKE   Ay, but she'll think that it is spoke in hate.
35 PROTEUS Ay, if his enemy deliver it:
            Therefore it must with circumstance be spoken
            By one whom she esteemeth as his friend.
DUKE   Then you must undertake to slander him.
PROTEUS   And that, my lord, I shall be loath to do:
40   'Tis an ill office for a gentleman,
            Especially against his very friend.
DUKE   Where your good word cannot advantage him,
            Your slander never can endamage him;
            Therefore the office is indifferent,
45   Being entreated to it by your friend.
PROTEUS   You have prevailed, my lord: if I can do it
            By aught that I can speak in his dispraise,
            She shall not long continue love to him.
            But say this weed her love from Valentine,
50   It follows not that she will love Sir Turio.
TURIO   Therefore, as you unwind her love from him,
            Lest it should ravel and be good to none,
            You must provide to bottom it on me,
            Which must be done by praising me as much
55   As you in worth dispraise Sir Valentine.
DUKE   And, Proteus, we dare trust you in this kind
            Because we know, on Valentine's report,
            You are already Love's firm votary,
            And cannot soon revolt and change your mind.

---

32 descent social status   **35 deliver** speak   **36 circumstance** detailed evidence   **39 loath**
very reluctant   **41 very** true   **45 friend** i.e. the duke   **47 aught . . . dispraise** anything that I
can say to damage his character   **49 weed** root out   **52 ravel** get tangled up   **53 provide**
prepare   **bottom** wind into a ball (Silvia's love is being imaged as thread being unwound from
Valentine and wound around Turio)   **56 kind** business

60 Upon this warrant shall you have access
Where you with Silvia may confer at large —
For she is lumpish, heavy, melancholy,
And, for your friend's sake, will be glad of you —
Where you may temper her by your persuasion
65 To hate young Valentine and love my friend.
PROTEUS   As much as I can do, I will effect.
But you, Sir Turio, are not sharp enough:
You must lay lime to tangle her desires
By wailful sonnets, whose composèd rhymes
70 Should be full-fraught with serviceable vows.
DUKE   Ay, much is the force of heaven-bred poesy.
PROTEUS   Say that upon the altar of her beauty
You sacrifice your tears, your sighs, your heart.
Write till your ink be dry, and with your tears
75 Moist it again, and frame some feeling line
That may discover such integrity:
For Orpheus' lute was strung with poets' sinews,
Whose golden touch could soften steel and stones,
Make tigers tame and huge leviathans
80 Forsake unsounded deeps to dance on sands.
After your dire-lamenting elegies,
Visit by night your lady's chamber-window
With some sweet consort; to their instruments
Tune a deploring dump. The night's dead silence
85 Will well become such sweet-complaining grievance.
This, or else nothing, will inherit her.
DUKE   This discipline shows thou hast been in love.

---

60 **warrant** authorization   62 **lumpish** dull/despondent   **heavy** gloomy   64 **temper** mold
67 **sharp** ardent, keen   68 **lime** birdlime, a sticky substance spread on branches to catch birds
tangle entangle, trap   69 **wailful sonnets** lamenting, wistful love poems   **composèd** carefully
constructed   70 **full-fraught . . . vows** entirely filled with vows of service   71 **heaven-bred**
poesy poetry inspired by heaven   75 **frame** compose   76 **discover** reveal   **integrity** absolute
devotion/total sincerity   77 **Orpheus** in Greek legend, a musician so skillful that his music
could even charm animals, rocks, and trees   **sinews** tendons   79 **leviathans** sea monsters
80 **Forsake unsounded deeps** abandon the unfathomed parts of the sea   81 **dire-lamenting**
deeply sorrowing   **elegies** mournful love poems   83 **consort** group of musicians   84 **Tune**
sing   **deploring** doleful   **dump** sorrowful melody   86 **inherit** gain possession of
87 **discipline** learning/teaching

TURIO	And thy advice this night I'll put in practice.
	Therefore, sweet Proteus, my direction-giver,
90	Let us into the city presently
	To sort some gentlemen well skilled in music.
	I have a sonnet that will serve the turn
	To give the onset to thy good advice.
DUKE	About it, gentlemen!
95 PROTEUS	We'll wait upon your grace till after supper,
	And afterward determine our proceedings.
DUKE	Even now about it. I will pardon you. *Exeunt*

Act 4 Scene 1

running scene 13

Enter certain Outlaws

FIRST OUTLAW	Fellows, stand fast: I see a passenger.
SECOND OUTLAW	If there be ten, shrink not, but down with 'em.

[*Enter Valentine and Speed*]

THIRD OUTLAW	Stand, sir, and throw us that you have about ye.
	If not, we'll make you sit and rifle you.
5 SPEED	Sir, we are undone; these are the villains
	That all the travellers do fear so much.
VALENTINE	My friends—
FIRST OUTLAW	That's not so, sir: we are your enemies.
SECOND OUTLAW	Peace: we'll hear him.
10 THIRD OUTLAW	Ay, by my beard, will we: for he is a proper man.
VALENTINE	Then know that I have little wealth to lose;
	A man I am, crossed with adversity:
	My riches are these poor habiliments,
	Of which, if you should here disfurnish me,
15	You take the sum and substance that I have.
SECOND OUTLAW	Whither travel you?

---

91 **sort** select   93 **give . . . to** bring about the initiation of   94 **About it** on with the business
97 **pardon you** i.e. from having to wait upon me   **4.1** *Location: wilderness/forest*
1 **passenger** traveler   3 **Stand** stop (**sit** in the following line plays on the sense of "remain standing")   4 **rifle** rob   10 **proper** fine-looking   12 **crossed with** thwarted by
13 **habiliments** clothes   14 **disfurnish** deprive   15 **sum and substance** everything

VALENTINE	To Verona.
FIRST OUTLAW	Whence came you?
VALENTINE	From Milan.

20 THIRD OUTLAW   Have you long sojourned there?

VALENTINE   Some sixteen months, and longer might have
    stayed,
    If crookèd fortune had not thwarted me.

FIRST OUTLAW   What, were you banished thence?

VALENTINE   I was.

25 SECOND OUTLAW   For what offence?

VALENTINE   For that which now torments me to rehearse:
    I killed a man, whose death I much repent,
    But yet I slew him manfully, in fight,
    Without false vantage or base treachery.

30 FIRST OUTLAW   Why, ne'er repent it, if it were done so;
    But were you banished for so small a fault?

VALENTINE   I was, and held me glad of such a doom.

SECOND OUTLAW   Have you the tongues?

VALENTINE   My youthful travel therein made me happy,
35   Or else I often had been miserable.

THIRD OUTLAW   By the bare scalp of Robin Hood's fat friar,
    This fellow were a king for our wild faction!

FIRST OUTLAW   We'll have him. Sirs, a word.   *Outlaws confer privately*

SPEED   Master, be one of them: it's an honourable kind of
40   thievery.

VALENTINE   Peace, villain.

SECOND OUTLAW   Tell us this: have you anything to take to?

VALENTINE   Nothing but my fortune.

THIRD OUTLAW   Know then that some of us are gentlemen,
45   Such as the fury of ungoverned youth
    Thrust from the company of awful men.

---

20 sojourned stayed   **22 crookèd** malign, devious   **29 false vantage** unfair advantage
32 held . . . doom was pleased to get such a (reasonable) sentence   **33 Have . . . tongues?** Can
you speak any foreign languages?   **34 happy** fortunate/accomplished   **36 fat friar** i.e. Friar
Tuck, a member of Robin Hood's band of outlaws   **37 were** would be (a good)   **faction** group
42 anything . . . to any resources   **45 ungoverned** uncontrolled, reckless, violent   **46 awful**
worthy of respect (or possibly a printer's error for "lawful")

Myself was from Verona banishèd
For practising to steal away a lady,
An heir and niece, allied unto the duke.
SECOND OUTLAW   And I from Mantua, for a gentleman, 50
Who, in my mood, I stabbed unto the heart.
FIRST OUTLAW   And I for such like petty crimes as these.
But to the purpose: for we cite our faults,
That they may hold excused our lawless lives;
And partly, seeing you are beautified 55
With goodly shape, and by your own report
A linguist and a man of such perfection
As we do in our quality much want—
SECOND OUTLAW   Indeed, because you are a banished man,
Therefore, above the rest, we parley to you: 60
Are you content to be our general?
To make a virtue of necessity
And live as we do in this wilderness?
THIRD OUTLAW   What say'st thou? Wilt thou be of our consort?
Say 'ay', and be the captain of us all: 65
We'll do thee homage and be ruled by thee,
Love thee as our commander and our king.
FIRST OUTLAW   But if thou scorn our courtesy, thou diest.
SECOND OUTLAW   Thou shalt not live to brag what we have
offered.
VALENTINE   I take your offer and will live with you, 70
Provided that you do no outrages
On silly women or poor passengers.
THIRD OUTLAW   No, we detest such vile base practices.
Come, go with us: we'll bring thee to our crews,
And show thee all the treasure we have got, 75
Which, with ourselves, all rest at thy dispose.   *Exeunt*

---

48 practising plotting   **49 niece** kinswoman (phrase sometimes emended to "An heir, and near allied")   **50 Mantua** northern Italian dukedom   **51 mood** rage   **53 cite** acknowledge/mention   **54 hold excused** explain/justify   **56 shape** appearance/figure   **58 quality** profession   **60 above the rest** for this reason above all   **parley** talk/negotiate   **64 consort** company/group   **66 do thee homage** perform acts of allegiance/acknowledge your superiority   **71 outrages** acts of violence   **72 silly** defenseless   **74 crews** gang   **76 dispose** disposal

Act 4 Scene 2

Enter Proteus

PROTEUS	Already have I been false to Valentine,
	And now I must be as unjust to Turio:
	Under the colour of commending him,
	I have access my own love to prefer.
5	But Silvia is too fair, too true, too holy,
	To be corrupted with my worthless gifts;
	When I protest true loyalty to her,
	She twits me with my falsehood to my friend;
	When to her beauty I commend my vows,
10	She bids me think how I have been forsworn
	In breaking faith with Julia, whom I loved;
	And notwithstanding all her sudden quips,
	The least whereof would quell a lover's hope,
	Yet, spaniel-like, the more she spurns my love,
15	The more it grows and fawneth on her still.

[Enter Turio and Musicians]

	But here comes Turio; now must we to her window,
	And give some evening music to her ear.
TURIO	How now, Sir Proteus, are you crept before us?
PROTEUS	Ay, gentle Turio, for you know that love
20	Will creep in service where it cannot go.
TURIO	Ay, but I hope, sir, that you love not here.
PROTEUS	Sir, but I do: or else I would be hence.
TURIO	Who, Silvia?
PROTEUS	Ay, Silvia: for your sake.
25 TURIO	I thank you for your own. Now, gentlemen,
	Let's tune, and to it lustily awhile.

[Enter, at a distance, the Host, and Julia in boy's clothes]   *They talk apart*

4.2 *Location: Milan*   3 colour pretext   **commending** praising   **7 protest** swear   **8 twits** taunts/reproaches   **9 commend** offer/declare   **12 quips** sharp retorts   **18 crept** moved quietly, stealthily   **20 creep** crawl   **go** walk upright   **21 love not here** i.e. do not love Silvia   **25 I . . . own** i.e. it's a good thing for your sake that you made your meaning clear   **26 lustily** heartily   ***Host*** innkeeper

HOST   Now, my young guest, methinks you're allicholly; I
pray you, why is it?

JULIA   Marry, mine host, because I cannot be merry.

30 HOST   Come, we'll have you merry: I'll bring you where
you shall hear music and see the gentleman that you asked
for.

JULIA   But shall I hear him speak?

HOST   Ay, that you shall.

35 JULIA .   That will be music.   *Music plays*

HOST   Hark, hark!

JULIA   Is he among these?

HOST   Ay: but peace, let's hear 'em.

[*PROTEUS or A MUSICIAN sings the*] song
        Who is Silvia? What is she?
40   That all our swains commend her?
        Holy, fair and wise is she:
        The heaven such grace did lend her,
            That she might admirèd be.
        Is she kind as she is fair?
45   For beauty lives with kindness:
        Love doth to her eyes repair,
        To help him of his blindness,
            And, being helped, inhabits there.
        Then to Silvia let us sing,
50   That Silvia is excelling;
        She excels each mortal thing
        Upon the dull earth dwelling.
            To her let us garlands bring.

HOST   How now? Are you sadder than you were before?
55 How do you, man? The music likes you not.

JULIA   You mistake: the musician likes me not.

HOST   Why, my pretty youth?

27 **allicholly** the Host means "melancholy"   **40 swains** youths/lovers   **42 grace**
virtue/favor/elegance   **43 admirèd** marveled at   **46 repair** hasten   **47 of** with   **55 do** are
likes pleases   **56 likes me not** does not please me/does not love me

	JULIA	He plays false, father.
	HOST	How, out of tune on the strings?
60	JULIA	Not so: but yet so false that he grieves my very heart-strings.
	HOST	You have a quick ear.
	JULIA	Ay, I would I were deaf: it makes me have a slow heart.
65	HOST	I perceive you delight not in music.
	JULIA	Not a whit, when it jars so.
	HOST	Hark what fine change is in the music.
	JULIA	Ay, that change is the spite.
	HOST	You would have them always play but one thing?
70	JULIA	I would always have one play but one thing.

JULIA But, host, doth this Sir Proteus that we talk on
Often resort unto this gentlewoman?

HOST I tell you what Lance his man told me: he loved her out of all nick.

75 JULIA Where is Lance?

HOST Gone to seek his dog, which tomorrow, by his master's command, he must carry for a present to his lady.

JULIA Peace, stand aside: the company parts.   *Julia and the*

PROTEUS Sir Turio, fear not you: I will so plead   *Host stand aside*

80 That you shall say my cunning drift excels.

TURIO Where meet we?

PROTEUS At Saint Gregory's well.

TURIO Farewell.   [*Exeunt Turio and Musicians*]

[*Enter Silvia above, at her window*]

PROTEUS Madam, good even to your ladyship.

---

58 **plays false** plays out of tune/is unfaithful   **father** respectful term for an old man
62 **quick** sharp (in the following line Julia plays on the sense of "lively, rapid" when she contrasts quick with **slow**)   63 **slow** heavy/not rapid   66 **jars** sounds discordant   67 **change** modulation (in the following line Julia plays on the sense of "fickle/unfaithful")   68 **spite** vexation   69 **but one thing** only the same melody   70 **one . . . thing** a lover play only one role (**play** is sexually suggestive and **thing** puns on "vagina")   74 **out . . . nick** beyond reckoning
82 **Saint Gregory's well** has been identified as an actual well near Milan

85	SILVIA	I thank you for your music, gentlemen.

SILVIA   I thank you for your music, gentlemen.
Who is that that spake?

PROTEUS   One, lady, if you knew his pure heart's truth,
You would quickly learn to know him by his voice.

SILVIA   Sir Proteus, as I take it.

PROTEUS   Sir Proteus, gentle lady, and your servant.

SILVIA   What's your will?

PROTEUS   That I may compass yours.

SILVIA   You have your wish: my will is even this,
That presently you hie you home to bed.
Thou subtle, perjured, false, disloyal man:
Think'st thou I am so shallow, so conceitless,
To be seduced by thy flattery,
That hast deceived so many with thy vows?
Return, return, and make thy love amends.
For me — by this pale queen of night I swear —
I am so far from granting thy request
That I despise thee for thy wrongful suit,
And by and by intend to chide myself,
Even for this time I spend in talking to thee.

PROTEUS   I grant, sweet love, that I did love a lady:
But she is dead.

JULIA   'Twere false, if I should speak it;   *Aside*
For I am sure she is not burièd.

SILVIA   Say that she be: yet Valentine thy friend
Survives; to whom, thyself art witness,
I am betrothed. And art thou not ashamed
To wrong him with thy importunacy?

PROTEUS   I likewise hear that Valentine is dead.

SILVIA   And so suppose am I: for in his grave
Assure thyself, my love is burièd.

---

91 will intent/desire   **92 compass yours** fulfill your wishes/win your approval/gain your
sexual desire   **94 hie** hurry   **95 subtle** cunning, treacherous   **96 conceitless** witless
99 thy love i.e. Julia   **100 pale . . . night** i.e. the moon (associated with chastity)
102 wrongful suit dishonorable/insulting courtship   **103 by and by** and for that reason/
presently   **107 if** even if   **112 importunacy** persistent entreaties   **114 And . . . I** in that case,
you may assume that I am too

	PROTEUS	Sweet lady, let me rake it from the earth.

PROTEUS   Sweet lady, let me rake it from the earth.

SILVIA   Go to thy lady's grave and call hers thence,
Or at the least, in hers sepulchre thine.

JULIA   He heard not that.   *Aside*

120 PROTEUS   Madam, if your heart be so obdurate,
Vouchsafe me yet your picture for my love,
The picture that is hanging in your chamber.
To that I'll speak, to that I'll sigh and weep:
For since the substance of your perfect self
125   Is else devoted, I am but a shadow,
And to your shadow will I make true love.

JULIA   If 'twere a substance, you would sure deceive it, *Aside*
And make it but a shadow, as I am.

SILVIA   I am very loath to be your idol, sir;
130 But, since your falsehood shall become you well
To worship shadows and adore false shapes,
Send to me in the morning, and I'll send it.
And so, good rest.

PROTEUS   As wretches have o'ernight
135 That wait for execution in the morn.

[Exeunt Proteus and Silvia, separately]

JULIA   Host, will you go?

HOST   By my halidom, I was fast asleep.

JULIA   Pray you, where lies Sir Proteus?

HOST   Marry, at my house. Trust me, I think 'tis almost
140 day.

JULIA   Not so: but it hath been the longest night
That e'er I watched, and the most heaviest.   *[Exeunt]*

---

117 hers i.e. her (Julia's) love   **118 sepulchre** bury   **120 obdurate** unyielding
121 Vouchsafe permit   **125 else** elsewhere   **126 shadow** image/portrait (playing on the
usual sense in the previous line)   **127 If . . . am** if the image in Silvia's picture was real, you
would be false to it and reduce it to mere shadowy unreality, just as you have done to me (Julia
is changed from her real self through both heartbreak and disguise)   **130 since . . . well** as it
will suit your fickle nature well   **137 halidom** all I consider holy   **138 lies** lodges   **139 house**
i.e. inn   **142 heaviest** sorrowful/darkest

Act 4 Scene 3

Enter Eglamour

EGLAMOUR   This is the hour that Madam Silvia
   Entreated me to call and know her mind:
   There's some great matter she'd employ me in.
   Madam, madam.

[*Enter Silvia above, at her window*]

5 SILVIA   Who calls?

EGLAMOUR Your servant and your friend;
   One that attends your ladyship's command.

SILVIA   Sir Eglamour, a thousand times good morrow.

EGLAMOUR As many, worthy lady, to yourself:

10   According to your ladyship's impose,
   I am thus early come to know what service
   It is your pleasure to command me in.

SILVIA   O, Eglamour, thou art a gentleman —
   Think not I flatter, for I swear I do not —

15   Valiant, wise, remorseful, well accomplished.
   Thou art not ignorant what dear good will
   I bear unto the banished Valentine,
   Nor how my father would enforce me marry
   Vain Turio, whom my very soul abhorred.

20   Thyself hast loved, and I have heard thee say
   No grief did ever come so near thy heart
   As when thy lady and thy true love died,
   Upon whose grave thou vowed'st pure chastity.
   Sir Eglamour, I would to Valentine,

25   To Mantua, where I hear he makes abode;
   And for the ways are dangerous to pass,
   I do desire thy worthy company,
   Upon whose faith and honour I repose.
   Urge not my father's anger, Eglamour,

4.3 *Eglamour amour* (French for "love") suggests a lover; his own lady having died, Eglamour remains devoted to the cause of true love by functioning as a knightly escort to Silvia
10 impose command **15 remorseful** compassionate **19 Vain** foolish **24 would** want to go
26 for because **28 repose** rely

30 But think upon my grief, a lady's grief,
And on the justice of my flying hence,
To keep me from a most unholy match,
Which heaven and fortune still rewards with plagues.
I do desire thee, even from a heart
35 As full of sorrows as the sea of sands,
To bear me company and go with me:
If not, to hide what I have said to thee,
That I may venture to depart alone.

EGLAMOUR   Madam, I pity much your grievances,
40 Which, since I know they virtuously are placed,
I give consent to go along with you,
Recking as little what betideth me
As much I wish all good befortune you.
When will you go?

45 SILVIA   This evening coming.

EGLAMOUR   Where shall I meet you?

SILVIA   At Friar Patrick's cell,
Where I intend holy confession.

EGLAMOUR   I will not fail your ladyship.
50 Good morrow, gentle lady.

SILVIA   Good morrow, kind Sir Eglamour.

Exeunt [separately]

Act 4 Scene 4

Enter Lance [with his dog, Crab]

LANCE   When a man's servant shall play the cur with him,
look you, it goes hard: one that I brought up of a puppy: one
that I saved from drowning, when three or four of his blind
brothers and sisters went to it. I have taught him, even as
5 one would say precisely, 'thus I would teach a dog'. I was sent
to deliver him as a present to Mistress Silvia from my master,

---

33 still always   **39 grievances** distress/sorrowful affections   **42 Recking** caring   **betideth**
befalls   **43 befortune** happen to   **47 cell** simple dwelling   **4.4**   **1 play the cur** play up/be
knavish/behave like a dog   **2 goes hard** is tough   **of** from

and I came no sooner into the dining-chamber but he steps
me to her trencher and steals her capon's leg: O, 'tis a foul
thing when a cur cannot keep himself in all companies. I
10   would have, as one should say, one that takes upon him to be
a dog indeed, to be, as it were, a dog at all things. If I had not
had more wit than he, to take a fault upon me that he did, I
think verily he had been hanged for't: sure as I live, he had
suffered for't, you shall judge. He thrusts me himself into the
15   company of three or four gentlemanlike dogs under the
duke's table: he had not been there — bless the mark — a
pissing while, but all the chamber smelt him. 'Out with the
dog!' says one. 'What cur is that?' says another. 'Whip him
out', says the third. 'Hang him up', says the duke. I, having
20   been acquainted with the smell before, knew it was Crab, and
goes me to the fellow that whips the dogs: 'Friend,' quoth I,
'you mean to whip the dog?' 'Ay, marry, do I', quoth he. 'You
do him the more wrong,' quoth I, ''twas I did the thing you
wot of.' He makes me no more ado, but whips me out of the
25   chamber. How many masters would do this for his servant?
Nay, I'll be sworn, I have sat in the stocks for puddings
he hath stolen, otherwise he had been executed: I have stood
on the pillory for geese he hath killed, otherwise he had
suffered for't.— Thou think'st not of this now. Nay,   *To Crab*
30   I remember the trick you served me when I took my leave of
Madam Silvia: did not I bid thee still mark me and do as I do?
When didst thou see me heave up my leg and make water
against a gentlewoman's farthingale? Didst thou ever see me
do such a trick?

[*Enter Proteus, and Julia disguised as Sebastian*]

---

7 **steps me** steps (**me** is emphatic)   8 **trencher** plate   **capon's** chicken's   9 **keep** control
10 **takes upon him** undertakes   11 **a dog at** adept at (puns on the literal meaning of **dog**)
12 **take . . . did** plead guilty to his wrongdoing   13 **verily** truly   **had** would have   14 **thrusts
me** thrusts   16 **bless the mark** i.e. pardon the phrase I am about to use   17 **pissing while**
short time (literally, the time it takes to urinate)   24 **wot of** have learned about   **makes . . .
ado** makes no more fuss   26 **stocks** contraption for public punishment in which a person had
their wrists and ankles confined   **puddings** sausages   28 **pillory** instrument of punishment
in which a person had their head and wrists confined   31 **still mark** always pay attention to
32 **heave up** raise   **make water** urinate

35   PROTEUS   Sebastian is thy name? I like thee well and will
            employ thee in some service presently.   *To Julia*

      JULIA   In what you please, I'll do what I can.

      PROTEUS   I hope thou wilt.— How now, you whoreson   *To Lance*
            peasant, where have you been these two days loitering?

40   LANCE   Marry, sir, I carried Mistress Silvia the dog you
            bade me.

      PROTEUS   And what says she to my little jewel?

      LANCE   Marry, she says your dog was a cur, and tells you
            currish thanks is good enough for such a present.

45   PROTEUS   But she received my dog?

      LANCE   No indeed did she not: here have I brought him back
            again.

      PROTEUS   What, didst thou offer her this from me?   *Points to Crab*

      LANCE   Ay, sir: the other squirrel was stolen from me by the
50   hangman boys in the market-place, and then I offered her
            mine own, who is a dog as big as ten of yours, and therefore
            the gift the greater.

      PROTEUS   Go get thee hence, and find my dog again,
            Or ne'er return again into my sight.

55   Away, I say: stay'st thou to vex me here?   [*Exit Lance with Crab*]
            A slave, that still an end turns me to shame.
            Sebastian, I have entertained thee,
            Partly that I have need of such a youth
            That can with some discretion do my business,
60   For 'tis no trusting to yond foolish lout,
            But chiefly for thy face and thy behaviour,
            Which, if my augury deceive me not,
            Witness good bringing up, fortune and truth:
            Therefore know thou, for this I entertain thee.
65   Go presently, and take this ring with thee,   *Gives a ring*

---

42 jewel i.e. the pretty dog Proteus thinks Lance delivered to Silvia   **43 cur** dog/ill-bred fellow
44 currish mean-spirited/snarling   **49 squirrel** i.e. small dog (contemptuous)   **50 hangman
boys** rascally boys fit for the hangman   **56 still an end** continuously (possible printer's error
for "on end")   **57 entertained** taken into service   **60 yond** yonder, the one over there, i.e.
Lance   **61 behaviour** bearing/manners   **62 augury** discernment/prediction   **63 Witness** are
evidence of

Deliver it to Madam Silvia;
She loved me well delivered it to me.

JULIA   It seems you loved not her, to leave her token:
She is dead, belike?

70   PROTEUS   Not so: I think she lives.

JULIA   Alas!

PROTEUS   Why dost thou cry 'Alas'?

JULIA   I cannot choose but pity her.

PROTEUS   Wherefore shouldst thou pity her?

75   JULIA   Because methinks that she loved you as well
As you do love your lady Silvia:
She dreams on him that has forgot her love,
You dote on her that cares not for your love.
'Tis pity love should be so contrary:

80   And thinking on it makes me cry 'Alas'.

PROTEUS   Well, give her that ring and therewithal
This letter. That's her chamber. Tell my lady   *Gives a letter*
I claim the promise for her heavenly picture.
Your message done, hie home unto my chamber,

85   Where thou shalt find me, sad and solitary.   [*Exit*]

JULIA   How many women would do such a message?
Alas, poor Proteus, thou hast entertained
A fox to be the shepherd of thy lambs.
Alas, poor fool, why do I pity him

90   That with his very heart despiseth me?
Because he loves her, he despiseth me:
Because I love him, I must pity him.
This ring I gave him when he parted from me,
To bind him to remember my good will.

95   And now am I, unhappy messenger,
To plead for that which I would not obtain,
To carry that which I would have refused,
To praise his faith which I would have dispraised.

---

67 delivered who gave   **68 leave** part with/forsake   **81 therewithal** with it   **89 poor fool**
Julia refers to herself   **96 To . . . obtain** i.e. Silvia's love (for Proteus)

I am my master's true-confirmèd love,
100 But cannot be true servant to my master,
Unless I prove false traitor to myself.
Yet will I woo for him, but yet so coldly
As, heaven it knows, I would not have him speed.

[*Enter Silvia, attended by her servant Ursula*]

Gentlewoman, good day: I pray you, be my mean
105 To bring me where to speak with Madam Silvia.

SILVIA   What would you with her, if that I be she?

JULIA   If you be she, I do entreat your patience
To hear me speak the message I am sent on.

SILVIA   From whom?

110 JULIA   From my master, Sir Proteus, madam.

SILVIA   O, he sends you for a picture?

JULIA   Ay, madam.

SILVIA   Ursula, bring my picture there.   *Ursula brings the picture*
Go give your master this: tell him from me,
115 One Julia, that his changing thoughts forget,
Would better fit his chamber than this shadow.

JULIA   Madam, please you peruse this letter.   *Gives her a letter*
Pardon me, madam, I have unadvised
Delivered you a paper that I should not:
120 This is the letter to your ladyship.   *Takes back the letter*

SILVIA   I pray thee, let me look on that again.   *and gives another*

JULIA   It may not be: good madam, pardon me.

SILVIA   There, hold.
I will not look upon your master's lines:
125 I know they are stuffed with protestations
And full of newfound oaths, which he will break
As easily as I do tear his paper.   *Tears the letter*

JULIA   Madam, he sends your ladyship this ring.   *Offers the ring*

SILVIA   The more shame for him that he sends it me,
130 For I have heard him say a thousand times

---

99 **true-confirmèd** truly established/legitimate/declared   103 **speed** succeed   104 **mean**
means/agent   106 **if . . . she** if I am indeed Silvia   116 **fit his chamber** suit his room
118 **unadvised** inadvertently   123 **hold** wait a moment   125 **protestations** declarations (of
love)   126 **newfound** recently invented

His Julia gave it him at his departure.
Though his false finger have profaned the ring,
Mine shall not do his Julia so much wrong.

JULIA   She thanks you.

135 SILVIA   What say'st thou?

JULIA   I thank you, madam, that you tender her.
Poor gentlewoman, my master wrongs her much.

SILVIA   Dost thou know her?

JULIA   Almost as well as I do know myself.

140 To think upon her woes, I do protest
That I have wept a hundred several times.

SILVIA   Belike she thinks that Proteus hath forsook her?

JULIA   I think she doth: and that's her cause of sorrow.

SILVIA   Is she not passing fair?

145 JULIA   She hath been fairer, madam, than she is:
When she did think my master loved her well,
She, in my judgement, was as fair as you.
But since she did neglect her looking-glass
And threw her sun-expelling mask away,

150 The air hath starved the roses in her cheeks
And pinched the lily-tincture of her face,
That now she is become as black as I.

SILVIA   How tall was she?

JULIA   About my stature: for at Pentecost,

155 When all our pageants of delight were played,
Our youth got me to play the woman's part,
And I was trimmed in Madam Julia's gown,
Which served me as fit, by all men's judgements,
As if the garment had been made for me:

160 Therefore I know she is about my height.
And at that time I made her weep a-good,

---

132 profaned abused/treated irreverently   136 tender care for/esteem   149 sun-expelling
mask mask worn by a lady to protect her complexion from the sun   151 pinched the lily-
tincture eroded the lily-white color   152 as . . . I Julia may have besmirched her face as part of
her disguise   154 stature height   Pentecost Whitsun, Christian festival held on the seventh
Sunday after Easter   155 pageants of delight enjoyable plays/entertainments
157 trimmed dressed up   161 a-good in earnest

For I did play a lamentable part.
Madam, 'twas Ariadne, passioning
For Theseus' perjury and unjust flight,
165 Which I so lively acted with my tears
That my poor mistress, movèd therewithal,
Wept bitterly: and would I might be dead
If I in thought felt not her very sorrow.

SILVIA   She is beholding to thee, gentle youth.
170 Alas, poor lady, desolate and left!
I weep myself to think upon thy words.
Here, youth, there is my purse: I give thee this   *Gives money*
For thy sweet mistress' sake, because thou lov'st her.
Farewell.   [*Exeunt Silvia and Ursula*]

175 **JULIA**   And she shall thank you for't, if e'er you know her.
A virtuous gentlewoman, mild and beautiful.
I hope my master's suit will be but cold,
Since she respects my mistress' love so much.
Alas, how love can trifle with itself!
180 Here is her picture: let me see, I think
If I had such a tire, this face of mine
Were full as lovely as is this of hers.
And yet the painter flattered her a little,
Unless I flatter with myself too much.
185 Her hair is auburn, mine is perfect yellow;
If that be all the difference in his love,
I'll get me such a coloured periwig.
Her eyes are grey as glass, and so are mine:
Ay, but her forehead's low, and mine's as high.
190 What should it be that he respects in her
But I can make respective in myself,

---

163 Ariadne . . . flight in Greek mythology Ariadne was abandoned by her lover **Theseus**
despite the fact that she had helped him to escape from the labyrinth that contained the beastly
Minotaur   **passioning** passionately sorrowing   **165 lively** in a lifelike way/convincingly
169 beholding indebted   **176 mild** gracious, kind   **177 suit . . . cold** wooing (of Silvia) will be
in vain/received coldly   **178 my mistress** i.e. Julia herself   **181 tire** headdress   **187 periwig**
wig   **189 as high** the same height as (i.e. no lower than) hers   **190 respects** values/admires
191 respective worthy of **respect**

If this fond Love were not a blinded god?
Come, shadow, come, and take this shadow up,
For 'tis thy rival.— O thou senseless form,   *Looks at the picture*
195   Thou shalt be worshipped, kissed, loved and adored;
And were there sense in his idolatry,
My substance should be statue in thy stead.
I'll use thee kindly, for thy mistress' sake
That used me so: or else, by Jove I vow,
200   I should have scratched out your unseeing eyes
To make my master out of love with thee.   *Exit*

Act 5 Scene 1

Enter Eglamour

EGLAMOUR   The sun begins to gild the western sky,
And now it is about the very hour
That Silvia, at Friar Patrick's cell, should meet me.
She will not fail; for lovers break not hours,
5   Unless it be to come before their time,
So much they spur their expedition.
See where she comes.—
[*Enter Silvia, with a mask*]
Lady, a happy evening!
SILVIA   Amen, amen. Go on, good Eglamour,
Out at the postern by the abbey-wall;
10   I fear I am attended by some spies.
EGLAMOUR   Fear not. The forest is not three leagues off:
If we recover that, we are sure enough.   *Exeunt*

---

193 **shadow** the disguised/heartbroken Julia   **take . . . up** pick up this picture/take on this
rival   194 **senseless form** unconscious image   197 **statue** i.e. an idol   **stead** place   198 **use**
treat   199 **Jove** king of the gods   **5.1 *Location: outside the city***   1 **gild** tinge with gold
4 **break not hours** do not fail to keep meetings   5 **before their time** early   6 **expedition** speedy
action   8 **Amen, amen** i.e. amen to that/yes indeed   9 **postern** side or back gate
10 **attended** followed   11 **three leagues** about nine miles   12 **recover** reach   **sure** secure

Act 5 Scene 2

Enter Turio, Proteus, [and] Julia [disguised as Sebastian]

	TURIO	Sir Proteus, what says Silvia to my suit?
	PROTEUS	O, sir, I find her milder than she was,
		And yet she takes exceptions at your person.
	TURIO	What? That my leg is too long?
5	PROTEUS	No, that it is too little.
	TURIO	I'll wear a boot, to make it somewhat rounder.
	JULIA	But love will not be spurred to what it loathes. *Aside*
	TURIO	What says she to my face?
	PROTEUS	She says it is a fair one.
10	TURIO	Nay then, the wanton lies: my face is black.
	PROTEUS	But pearls are fair; and the old saying is,
		Black men are pearls in beauteous ladies' eyes.
	JULIA	'Tis true, such pearls as put out ladies' eyes, *Aside*
		For I had rather wink than look on them.
15	TURIO	How likes she my discourse?
	PROTEUS	Ill, when you talk of war.
	TURIO	But well, when I discourse of love and peace.
	JULIA	But better indeed, when you hold your peace. *Aside*
	TURIO	What says she to my valour?
20	PROTEUS	O, sir, she makes no doubt of that.
	JULIA	She needs not, when she knows it cowardice. *Aside*
	TURIO	What says she to my birth?
	PROTEUS	That you are well derived.
	JULIA	True: from a gentleman to a fool. *Aside*
25	TURIO	Considers she my possessions?
	PROTEUS	O ay, and pities them.
	TURIO	Wherefore?

5.2 Location: *Milan*   2 milder more gracious, gentler   **3 person** physical appearance
5 little thin   **7 spurred** urged on (plays on the idea of the spurs of a riding-**boot**)   **9 fair**
attractive/pale-complexioned/effeminate   **10 wanton** willful, capricious woman   **black**
tanned   **13 pearls** cataracts/syphilitic sores   **put out** make useless   **eyes** eyes/vaginas
(syphilis infected both the eyes and the genitals)   **16 Ill . . . war** i.e. she does not like it when
you talk of violence/your talk of war only reminds her of your inadequacy for masculine
pursuits   **18 hold your peace** remain silent   **20 makes** has   **22 birth** noble ancestry
23 derived descended   **26 pities** is concerned for/considers pitiful

	JULIA	That such an ass should owe them.	*Aside*
	PROTEUS	That they are out by lease.	
30	JULIA	Here comes the duke.	

[*Enter the Duke*]

	DUKE	How now, Sir Proteus; how now, Turio.
		Which of you saw Eglamour of late?
	TURIO	Not I.
	PROTEUS	Nor I.
35	DUKE	Saw you my daughter?
	PROTEUS	Neither.
	DUKE	Why then,

She's fled unto that peasant Valentine,
And Eglamour is in her company.
40 'Tis true, for Friar Laurence met them both
As he, in penance, wandered through the forest.
Him he knew well, and guessed that it was she,
But, being masked, he was not sure of it.
Besides, she did intend confession
45 At Patrick's cell this even, and there she was not.
These likelihoods confirm her flight from hence.
Therefore I pray you stand not to discourse,
But mount you presently and meet with me
Upon the rising of the mountain-foot
50 That leads toward Mantua, whither they are fled:
Dispatch, sweet gentlemen, and follow me.   [*Exit*]

TURIO   Why, this it is to be a peevish girl,
That flies her fortune when it follows her.
I'll after, more to be revenged on Eglamour
55 Than for the love of reckless Silvia.   [*Exit*]

PROTEUS   And I will follow, more for Silvia's love
Than hate of Eglamour that goes with her.   [*Exit*]

---

28 owe own   **29 out by lease** rented out/not entirely in one's possession   **40 Friar Laurence** possibly a slip for **Friar Patrick**, the friar at whose cell Silvia and Eglamour met, though conceivably another friar is being referred to   **42 Him** i.e. Eglamour   **43 being masked** she having on a mask   **45 even** evening   **47 stand** delay   **48 mount you** rise up/get on horseback   **51 Dispatch** hurry up   **53 flies her fortune** flees her good fortune (i.e. Turio's courtship)   **55 reckless** uncaring

JULIA   And I will follow, more to cross that love
           Than hate for Silvia, that is gone for love.   *Exit*

Act 5 Scene 3

[*Enter*] *Silvia* [*with the*] *Outlaws*

FIRST OUTLAW   Come, come, be patient:
           We must bring you to our captain.
           SILVIA   A thousand more mischances than this one
           Have learned me how to brook this patiently.
5   SECOND OUTLAW   Come, bring her away.
           FIRST OUTLAW   Where is the gentleman that was with her?
           THIRD OUTLAW   Being nimble-footed, he hath outrun us.
           But Moyses and Valerius follow him.
           Go thou with her to the west end of the wood,
10   There is our captain: we'll follow him that's fled.
           The thicket is beset, he cannot scape.
                                        [*Exeunt Second and Third Outlaws*]
           FIRST OUTLAW   Come, I must bring you to our captain's cave.
           Fear not: he bears an honourable mind,
           And will not use a woman lawlessly.
15   SILVIA   O Valentine, this I endure for thee!   *Exeunt*

Act 5 Scene 4

Enter Valentine

VALENTINE   How use doth breed a habit in a man!
           This shadowy desert, unfrequented woods,
           I better brook than flourishing peopled towns:
           Here can I sit alone, unseen of any,
5   And to the nightingale's complaining notes
           Tune my distresses and record my woes.

5.3 *Location: wilderness/forest*   3 more mischances greater misfortunes   **4 brook** endure
8 Moyses and Valerius i.e. two of the outlaws ("**Moyses**" is a form of "Moses")   **11 beset**
surrounded/beseiged   **5.4   1 use** custom   **2 desert** deserted place   **5 complaining**
sorrowing   **6 record** sing

O thou that dost inhabit in my breast,
Leave not the mansion so long tenantless,
Lest, growing ruinous, the building fall
10   And leave no memory of what it was.
Repair me with thy presence, Silvia:
Thou gentle nymph, cherish thy forlorn swain.   *Commotion within*
What hallowing and what stir is this today?
These are my mates, that make their wills their law,
15   Have some unhappy passenger in chase.
They love me well: yet I have much to do
To keep them from uncivil outrages.
Withdraw thee, Valentine: who's this comes here?   *Stands aside*
[*Enter Proteus, Silvia, and Julia disguised as Sebastian*]
PROTEUS   Madam, this service I have done for you —
20   Though you respect not aught your servant doth —
To hazard life and rescue you from him
That would have forced your honour and your love..
Vouchsafe me for my meed but one fair look:
A smaller boon than this I cannot beg,
25   And less than this I am sure you cannot give.
VALENTINE   How like a dream is this? I see and hear: *Aside*
Love, lend me patience to forbear awhile.
SILVIA   O miserable, unhappy that I am!
PROTEUS   Unhappy were you, madam, ere I came:
30   But by my coming I have made you happy.
SILVIA   By thy approach thou mak'st me most unhappy.
JULIA   And me, when he approacheth to your presence. *Aside*
SILVIA   Had I been seizèd by a hungry lion,
I would have been a breakfast to the beast
35   Rather than have false Proteus rescue me.
O, heaven, be judge how I love Valentine,

---

8 mansion i.e. his breast, love's dwelling place   **11 Repair** revive (plays on the senses
"reconstruct" and "return")   **12 nymph** beautiful one/semi-divine being   **13 hallowing**
shouting   **15 Have** who have   **17 from** from committing   **20 respect** value   **aught**
anything   **21 him** i.e. the First Outlaw   **22 forced . . . love** i.e. sexually assaulted/raped you
23 Vouchsafe grant   **meed** reward   **fair** favorable/beautiful   **24 boon** favor
31 approach loving advances

Whose life's as tender to me as my soul!
And full as much, for more there cannot be,
I do detest false perjured Proteus.

40 Therefore be gone, solicit me no more.

PROTEUS   What dangerous action, stood it next to death,
Would I not undergo for one calm look:
O, 'tis the curse in love, and still approved,
When women cannot love where they're beloved.

45 SILVIA   When Proteus cannot love where he's beloved.
Read over Julia's heart, thy first best love,
For whose dear sake thou didst then rend thy faith
Into a thousand oaths; and all those oaths
Descended into perjury, to love me.

50 Thou hast no faith left now, unless thou'dst two,
And that's far worse than none: better have none
Than plural faith, which is too much by one.
Thou counterfeit to thy true friend!

PROTEUS   In love

55 Who respects friend?

SILVIA   All men but Proteus.

PROTEUS   Nay, if the gentle spirit of moving words
Can no way change you to a milder form,
I'll woo you like a soldier, at arms' end,

60 And love you 'gainst the nature of love: force ye.   *He grabs her*

SILVIA   O heaven!

PROTEUS   I'll force thee yield to my desire.

VALENTINE   Ruffian, let go that rude uncivil touch,   *Comes forward*
Thou friend of an ill fashion!

65 PROTEUS   Valentine!

---

37 **tender** precious   38 **full** just   40 **solicit** urge/chase after favors   41 **action** course of
action/fighting   43 **still approved** continually tested/proven   47 **rend** tear up   **faith**
promises, fidelity   50 **thou'dst two** i.e. you are somehow able to be a faithful lover to two
women at once   53 **counterfeit . . . friend** false imitation of a **true friend** like Valentine
55 **respects** takes into consideration   57 **spirit** nature/breath of air (this latter sense, picked
up on in **moving**, implies proximity between Silvia and Proteus)   **moving** wooing/stirring
58 **form** manner of behaving/appearance   59 **at arms' end** at sword's point/with my penis
63 **uncivil** uncivilized, brutish   64 **ill fashion** wicked sort

VALENTINE   Thou common friend, that's without faith or love,
For such is a friend now. Treacherous man,
Thou hast beguiled my hopes; nought but mine eye
Could have persuaded me. Now I dare not say
70 I have one friend alive: thou wouldst disprove me.
Who should be trusted, when one's right hand
Is perjured to the bosom? Proteus,
I am sorry I must never trust thee more,
But count the world a stranger for thy sake.
75 The private wound is deepest. O time most accurst,
'Mongst all foes that a friend should be the worst!
PROTEUS   My shame and guilt confounds me.
Forgive me, Valentine: if hearty sorrow
Be a sufficient ransom for offence,
80 I tender't here. I do as truly suffer
As e'er I did commit.
VALENTINE   Then I am paid:
And once again I do receive thee honest.
Who by repentance is not satisfied
85 Is nor of heaven nor earth, for these are pleased:
By penitence th'Eternal's wrath's appeased.
And that my love may appear plain and free,
All that was mine in Silvia I give thee.
JULIA   O, me unhappy!   *Swoons*
90 PROTEUS   Look to the boy.
VALENTINE   Why, boy! Why, wag! How now? What's the matter?
Look up: speak.
JULIA   O, good sir, my master charged me to deliver a ring
to Madam Silvia, which, out of my neglect, was never done.
95 PROTEUS   Where is that ring, boy?
JULIA   Here 'tis: this is it.   *Produces her own ring*

---

66 **common** commonplace (i.e. showing no special qualities of friendship)   68 **beguiled**
deceived   71 **right hand** i.e. his closest friend, Proteus   74 **count** consider   75 **private**
personal/internal   77 **confounds** overcomes   80 **tender't** offer it   81 **commit** do wrong
83 **receive thee** regard you as   84 **Who** he who   85 **nor** neither   **these** i.e. heaven and earth
86 **penitence** repentance   **th'Eternal's** God's   87 **love** i.e. friendship   **free** generous   91 **wag**
lad   93 **charged** instructed

PROTEUS   How? Let me see. Why, this is the ring I   *Takes ring*
    gave to Julia.

JULIA   O, cry you mercy, sir, I have mistook:

100   This is the ring you sent to Silvia.   *Offers another ring*

PROTEUS   But how cam'st thou by this ring? At my depart I
    gave this unto Julia.

JULIA   And Julia herself did give it me,
    And Julia herself hath brought it hither.   *Reveals herself*

105   PROTEUS   How? Julia?

JULIA   Behold her that gave aim to all thy oaths,
    And entertained 'em deeply in her heart.
    How oft hast thou with perjury cleft the root!
    O Proteus, let this habit make thee blush.

110   Be thou ashamed that I have took upon me
    Such an immodest raiment, if shame live
    In a disguise of love!
    It is the lesser blot, modesty finds,
    Women to change their shapes than men their minds.

115   PROTEUS   Than men their minds? 'Tis true. O heaven, were
    man
    But constant, he were perfect. That one error
    Fills him with faults, makes him run through all th'sins:
    Inconstancy falls off ere it begins.
    What is in Silvia's face but I may spy

120   More fresh in Julia's, with a constant eye?

VALENTINE   Come, come, a hand from either.   *Proteus and Julia*
    Let me be blest to make this happy close: *join hands*
    'Twere pity two such friends should be long foes.

PROTEUS   Bear witness, heaven, I have my wish forever.

125   JULIA   And I mine.

---

99 cry you mercy forgive me   **101 depart** departure (from Verona)   **106 gave aim** was the object of   **107 entertained** received   **108 cleft the root** split the bottom of my heart   **109 habit** outfit (Julia's page disguise; also puns on the sense of "behavior")   **111 raiment** clothing   **if . . . love** if it is in fact shameful to disguise oneself for love/if you can feel shame, being a false lover   **113 It . . . minds** propriety considers it less disgraceful for women to disguise themselves than for men to be unfaithful   **118 Inconstancy . . . begins** unfaithful passions drop away even before they begin

[*Enter Outlaws, with Duke and Turio*]

OUTLAWS   A prize, a prize, a prize!

VALENTINE   Forbear, forbear, I say! It is my lord the Duke.   *Outlaws*
      Your grace is welcome to a man disgraced,   *release Duke and Turio*
      Banished Valentine.

130 DUKE   Sir Valentine?

TURIO   Yonder is Silvia, and Silvia's mine.   *Steps forward*

VALENTINE   Turio, give back, or else embrace thy death: *Draws his*
      Come not within the measure of my wrath.   *sword*
      Do not name Silvia thine: if once again,
135   Verona shall not hold thee. Here she stands,
      Take but possession of her with a touch:
      I dare thee but to breathe upon my love.

TURIO   Sir Valentine, I care not for her, I.
      I hold him but a fool that will endanger
140   His body for a girl that loves him not:
      I claim her not, and therefore she is thine.

DUKE   The more degenerate and base art thou
      To make such means for her as thou hast done,
      And leave her on such slight conditions.
145   Now, by the honour of my ancestry,
      I do applaud thy spirit, Valentine,
      And think thee worthy of an empress' love:
      Know then, I here forget all former griefs,
      Cancel all grudge, repeal thee home again,
150   Plead a new state in thy unrivalled merit,
      To which I thus subscribe: Sir Valentine,
      Thou art a gentleman and well derived,
      Take thou thy Silvia, for thou hast deserved her.

VALENTINE   I thank your grace: the gift hath made me happy.
155   I now beseech you, for your daughter's sake,
      To grant one boon that I shall ask of you.

---

128 **disgraced** dishonored (plays on the sense of "out of favor")   132 **give** move
133 **measure** range   135 **hold** protect ("**Verona**" may be a slip for "Milan," which is Turio's
home)   143 **means** efforts   144 **slight conditions** insubstantial grounds   149 **repeal** recall
150 **Plead . . . merit** argue that there is a new state of affairs now that you have shown your
superior deserving   151 **subscribe** bear witness/acknowledge

DUKE	I grant it, for thine own, whate'er it be.
VALENTINE	These banished men that I have kept withal

Are men endued with worthy qualities:
160 Forgive them what they have committed here
And let them be recalled from their exile:
They are reformèd, civil, full of good,
And fit for great employment, worthy lord.

DUKE Thou hast prevailed: I pardon them and thee.
165 Dispose of them as thou know'st their deserts.
Come, let us go: we will include all jars
With triumphs, mirth and rare solemnity.

VALENTINE And as we walk along, I dare be bold
With our discourse to make your grace to smile.
170 What think you of this page, my lord?

DUKE I think the boy hath grace in him: he blushes.

VALENTINE I warrant you, my lord, more grace than boy.

DUKE What mean you by that saying?

VALENTINE Please you, I'll tell you as we pass along,
175 That you will wonder what hath fortunèd.
Come Proteus, 'tis your penance but to hear
The story of your loves discoverèd.
That done, our day of marriage shall be yours,
One feast, one house, one mutual happiness.   *Exeunt*

---

158 **kept withal** lived with   163 **employment** service   165 **Dispose of** make arrangements for **as . . . deserts** in accordance with their deservings   166 **include all jars** bring to an end, shut up all discord   167 **triumphs** festivities   **rare solemnity** marvelous celebration   171 **grace** virtue/charm   172 **grace** ideal female beauty   175 **fortunèd** come to pass

TEXTUAL NOTES

F = First Folio text of 1623, the only authority for the play
F2 = a correction introduced in the Second Folio text of 1632
Ed = a correction introduced by a later editor
SD = stage direction

List of parts *based on "Names of all the Actors" (reordered) at end of* F *text*

F *spells* Protheus, Thurio, Panthino

All entrances mid-scene = Ed. F *groups names of all characters in each scene at beginning of scene*
1.1.26 swam *spelled* swom *in* F **44 eating love** = F. *Some eds emend to* doting love **65 leave** = Ed. F = loue **67 metamorphosed** *spelled* metamorphis'd *in* F **78 a sheep** = F2. F = sheep **138 testerned** = F2. F = cestern'd
1.2.101 your = F2. F = you
1.3.17 travel *spelled* trauaile *in* F *which could mean either* travel *or* travail **89 father** = F2. F = Fathers
2.4.105 worthy = F2. F = worthy a **198 Is it** = F2. F = It is **mine eye** = Ed. F = mine **216 SD** *Exit* = F2. F = *Exeunt*
2.5.36 that = F2. F = that that
2.6.0 SD *alone* F = *solus*
3.1.56 tenor = Ed. F = tenure **278 master's ship** = Ed. F = Mastership **314 kissed fasting** = Ed. F = fasting
3.2.14 grievously = F *(corrected).* F *(uncorrected)* = heauily
4.1.35 often had been = F2. F = often had beene often
4.2.114 his = F2. F = her
4.3.42 Recking = Ed. F = Wreaking
4.4.50 hangman = Ed. F = Hangmans **64 thou** = F2. F = thee **68 to leave** = F2. F = not leaue
5.2.18 your = Ed. F = you

SCENE-BY-SCENE ANALYSIS

ACT 1 SCENE 1

The two friends Valentine and Proteus are discussing Valentine's imminent departure for Milan while Proteus is to stay in Verona and woo his beloved Julia. Valentine leaves and his servant Speed arrives hurrying after his master. Proteus asks him whether he delivered a letter he had written to Julia. Speed confirms that he has but gives a deliberately misleading account of her response to the letter in his attempt to gain payment from Proteus for delivering it. He departs and Proteus fears that Julia will disregard his letter because of the incompetent messenger.

ACT 1 SCENE 2

Lines 1–67: Julia is discussing love with Lucetta, asking which of her many suitors she favors. They list them but Lucetta initially refuses to pass judgment on Proteus. Finally she admits she thinks he loves Julia best and produces a letter for her mistress. She believes it is from Proteus and Julia is furious that Lucetta has accepted it and angrily dismisses her, telling her to take the letter with her. Lucetta leaves with the letter. Once alone Julia regrets not having looked at it, believing Lucetta should have made her. She attributes her own "wayward" behavior to the effect of "foolish love." She also repents sending Lucetta away pretending to be angry when in reality she was delighted and as penance calls Lucetta back.

Lines 68–144: Lucetta reappears and Julia demands to know what paper she has dropped and picked up. They quarrel over it and Julia seizes the letter and in her anger tears it to shreds, dismissing Lucetta once again. Lucetta departs but is not deceived, believing that Julia would be delighted with another letter. Alone again, Julia picks up the pieces and reads the fragments; finding her own name and Proteus', she folds them together so that they may "kiss, embrace, contend, do what you will." She is called away when Lucetta announces that dinner is ready and her father waiting.

ACT 1 SCENE 3

Lines 1–44: Antonio and Pantino are discussing Proteus. Pantino says that Antonio's brother is surprised that Antonio should allow his son to stay at home rather than send him abroad to see the world and broaden his mind. Antonio also thinks it would do his son good to gain some experience of the world, and when Pantino suggests sending Proteus to Valentine at the court of the duke of Milan, he agrees. They decide he should accompany a group of courtiers due to set out the following day.

Lines 45–92: Proteus enters, poring over a love letter from Julia. When his father demands to see it, he pretends it is a note from Valentine. His father wants to know what it says and Proteus says that he reports he's enjoying himself and wishes Proteus were there too. Antonio asks him how he feels about the idea. Proteus replies dutifully that his father's wishes are more important than his own. Antonio says in that case he can go to Milan the next day. Proteus tries to play for time, saying he needs to prepare himself, but Antonio dismisses the idea and says whatever he needs can be sent on, that his departure is already decided. He and Pantino leave. Proteus, now alone, realizes that he has brought this situation on himself: he concealed the letter from his father, fearing his disapproval, and now he will have to leave Julia anyway. Considering the sudden reversals of fortune in love, he likens it to the "uncertain glory of an April day."

ACT 2 SCENE 1

Lines 1–86: A comic scene between Valentine and Speed: Speed finds a glove he believes is Valentine's, who recognizes it belongs to Silvia. When he says her name, Speed calls her, much to Valentine's annoyance. Valentine asks Speed if he knows who she is and Speed inquires if he means the one "your worship loves." When Valentine asks him how he knows that he's in love, Speed replies that he's now like Proteus and shows all the external signs of a lover: he's melancholy, weeps, sighs, walks alone, and has lost his appetite. He's completely changed and is now unrecognizable from his former self. Valentine asks if all these signs are perceived in him and Speed says they're obvious for anyone to see. Valentine inquires again if Speed knows Silvia and describes her beauty, but in a battle of wits between the two, Speed contrives to continually misunderstand his meaning and deflate Valentine's praise of his beloved. Valentine tells Speed that Silvia has asked him to write "some lines to one she loves."

Lines 87–159: Silvia enters and she and Valentine greet one another effusively. Speed watches and comments on their encounter in a series of satirical asides. Valentine tells Silvia that he has dutifully written the letter that she asked him to write, although it pained him to do so and it was difficult since he did not know to whom it was written. She asks him if it was too much effort, but he replies that to please her he'd write "a thousand times as much." She tells him to take the letter back, and when he objects that it's for her, she says that she asked for it to be written, but it's not for herself but for him and, insisting he keep the letter, she leaves. Speed at once realizes that Silvia's playing a game with Valentine and that she's asked him to write a love letter from her to himself. Valentine wants to know what he's talking about and Speed tries to explain but Valentine is unconvinced.

ACT 2 SCENE 2

Proteus and Julia say goodbye before he leaves for Milan. They exchange rings and a kiss. Proteus protests that he will think of Julia every day and asks that something terrible should happen to him if he should forget his love.

ACT 2 SCENE 3

Lance, who is going to Milan with Proteus, explains that he has been bidding his sorrowful farewells to his family. They have all been upset and weeping except Crab, his dog, who did not "shed one tear." He goes through a comic recital of the whole family's responses, using a pair of shoes, a staff, and a hat. Crab, however, remained unmoved throughout. Pantino arrives telling him to hurry and not miss the tide, but Lance replies that if the river were dry he could fill it with his tears.

ACT 2 SCENE 4

Lines 1–96: Valentine and Turio compete for Silvia's love and attention. Her father, the Duke, arrives and asks Valentine if he knows Don Antonio and whether he has a son. Valentine confirms that he knows them both and goes on to praise his friend Proteus. The Duke tells him that in that case he will be pleased to know that Proteus has arrived. Valentine says that's all he would have wished for and the Duke tells Silvia and Turio to welcome him "according to his worth." He leaves, saying he'll send Proteus along to them. Valentine then confirms to Silvia that this is the friend he had talked of who would have accompanied him had it not been for his eyes being held prisoner by the looks of his beloved. Silvia thinks that she must have set him free or exchanged his eyes for some other pledge of loyalty or found a new lover since he has now left her to come to Milan, but Valentine does not believe this possible.

Lines 97–141: Proteus arrives and is welcomed by Valentine and introduced to Silvia. Valentine asks her to accept Proteus as her servant like himself. After some courtly banter, she accepts his service. She is then called away to her father. Valentine inquires after all their mutual friends back in Verona and asks after his lady and how his love thrives. Proteus says he used to be bored with talk of love and Valentine confesses that that's all changed. He is punished for having scorned love in the past and is now suffering all its pains and torments. He can think of nothing else but love.

Lines 142–216: Proteus guesses that Silvia is his "idol" and Valentine starts to praise her. Proteus, however, claims that his own beloved Julia is superior and the two vie with each other over the qualities of their respective ladies. Valentine tells Proteus that Silvia returns his love but unfortunately her father favors Turio as a suitor because of his great wealth. He then confides that they plan to elope that night. He is to climb to her bedroom window using a rope ladder down which they will escape. He asks Proteus to go with him to advise him. Proteus says he'll be along soon. Once alone he confesses that he's now fallen in love with Silvia. He will try to overcome his "erring love" but if he can't, he'll do everything possible to achieve her.

ACT 2 SCENE 5

Speed welcomes Lance to Padua—most likely to confuse the slower-witted Lance. The two hold a comic dialogue in which Speed tries to ascertain whether Proteus and Julia are to be married. Lance won't answer directly but says that his dog will answer for him. Speed says that his master is now become a "notable lover" too. The pair continue their comedy routine as they set off for the alehouse.

ACT 2 SCENE 6

A lengthy soliloquy in which Proteus debates whether or not to pursue Silvia. He justifies himself, arguing that if he does he will lose Valentine and Julia, but if he doesn't he will lose himself and, since he loves himself more than his friend, he resolves to "forget that Julia is alive," consider Valentine "an enemy," and pursue his love for Silvia. He decides, therefore, to betray Valentine's plan to elope with her to the Duke so that Valentine will be banished. He will then think of some way to thwart the dull-witted Turio, her father's preferred suitor, calling on "Love" to lend him "wings" to enable him to carry out his schemes swiftly.

ACT 2 SCENE 7

Lines 1–38: Back in Verona Julia asks for Lucetta's help with her plan to go to Proteus in Milan. Lucetta argues that it's a long, hard journey but Julia says it won't be with "Love's wings" to help her reach one so perfect as Proteus. Lucetta advises that it's better to wait for him to return, but Julia claims she'll starve to death without seeing him and that Lucetta might as well try to make a fire from snow as put out "the fire of love with words." Lucetta objects that she isn't trying to put out her "love's hot fire," just to keep it within the "bounds of reason," but Julia says that's impossible, she'll never rest until she finds her love.

Lines 39–90: Lucetta then turns to practical matters, asking her what she's going to wear. Julia says she'll disguise herself as a young man to avoid attracting unwelcome sexual attention. Lucetta tells her she should cut her hair, but Julia decides she'll tie it up. They discuss trousers and whether Julia needs a "codpiece." Julia is impatient over these details, although Lucetta gets great comedy mileage out of them. Julia then considers how scandalous her actions are and Lucetta advises her to stay at home, but Julia is determined. Lucetta says it doesn't matter as long as Proteus is pleased to see her, but she doubts that he will be. Julia, however, assures her that is the least of her "fear." His many oaths and tears are guarantees of his love. Lucetta points out that false men use these, but Julia defends Proteus. Lucetta says she hopes Julia's proved right when she finds him. Julia begs her not to think harshly of Proteus and to help her prepare for her journey and she'll leave everything behind in Lucetta's hands.

ACT 3 SCENE 1

Lines 1–50: Proteus tells the Duke of Valentine's plans to elope with Silvia that night, claiming that his actions are inspired by gratitude and his sense of duty. The Duke thanks him for his "honest care" and says that he has noticed that Valentine loves Silvia and now locks her in a high tower at night, keeping the key himself. Proteus tells him that they plan to escape via a rope ladder that Valentine has gone to fetch and that if he stays there he can "intercept" him. He begs that the Duke will keep his part in betraying his friend's secret, though, and the Duke willingly agrees. Proteus leaves as he sees Valentine coming.

Lines 51–170: Valentine enters and the Duke asks him where he's going so fast. Valentine says just to send letters to a friend and the Duke says in that case he can stay to listen to his problems. The Duke tells him that he wants Silvia to marry Turio but she's being stubborn and disobedient so that he doesn't love her anymore and that he's decided to remarry in his old age. He then concocts a story about having fallen in love with a woman whose family want her to marry someone else and asks Valentine's advice about wooing her. Valentine suggests sending presents and visiting her by night, and finally suggests that the Duke needs a rope ladder, which he can get for him. He will need a cloak to conceal the ladder. The Duke asks what sort of cloak and suggests one such as Valentine's. He removes it, finds the rope ladder and a letter addressed "To Silvia." The Duke reads Valentine's poem to Silvia. He is furious, banishes Valentine, and departs.

Lines 171–365: Valentine says he would prefer death to banishment but now must flee for his life. Proteus and Lance come to find him. His banishment has been proclaimed publicly. Valentine wants to know if Silvia has heard and Proteus describes her tearful reaction, but that despite her tears and pleas her father has refused to relent. He advises him to be positive and promises to deliver his letters to Silvia. Valentine asks Lance to send Speed to him and leaves with Proteus. Lance says that he may be a fool but he thinks Proteus a "kind of a knave" (villain). He then goes on to say that no one can say he's in love and yet he is, recounting all the "qualities" of his beloved. Speed arrives and after a prolonged discussion of Lance's lady and whether Speed can read, he finally tells him that Valentine is waiting for him.

ACT 3 SCENE 2

The Duke reassures Turio that now that Valentine has gone she will love him in time. Proteus enters and confirms that Valentine has left. The Duke asks him how to make Silvia forget Valentine and love Turio. Proteus suggests slandering him and undertakes to do it to promote a match between Silvia and Turio. The Duke says they can trust Proteus because they know he already loves another. Proteus recommends that Turio write her poetry and play music under Silvia's window. Turio decides to take his advice and to go that night.

ACT 4 SCENE 1

Valentine and Speed are ambushed by Outlaws. Valentine tells them that he has no money and has been banished from Milan for killing a man. They like the look of him and ask him to join them and become their "captain." He agrees, provided they "do no outrages" on defenseless women or travelers.

ACT 4 SCENE 2

Lines 1–84: Proteus confesses that he has already been false to Valentine and is now deceiving Turio since under cover of helping him woo Silvia, he is advancing his own suit, but she continually spurns his advances and accuses him of disloyalty to Valentine and Julia. The more she spurns him, though, the more he desires her. Turio arrives with the musicians to play under Silvia's window. Julia, disguised as a boy, enters at a distance with the Host who asks her why she is sad. He says he'll bring her to the young gentleman she's seeking and she'll hear music. They listen to the song addressed to Silvia. This makes Julia even more sad and when it's ended she asks if Proteus often visits Silvia. The Host says that according to Lance, he's in love with her. They stand aside and Proteus tells Turio that he will plead for him.

Lines 85–142: When Turio and the Musicians depart and Silvia comes to her window, Proteus attempts to woo her for himself. But Silvia is resolute, calling him "subtle, perjured, false, disloyal man" and telling him that she despises him. Proteus claims that Julia is dead but Silvia says, even so, Valentine is alive. Proteus says that he's dead too, in which case Silvia says, so is she, since her love is buried with him. Proteus begs for a picture of her at least and she says that since he worships "shadows," she'll send him her picture in the morning. When they've both departed, Julia calls the Host to go and asks where Proteus lodges. The Host confirms that he lodges at his house, saying that it's almost day, but Julia replies that it's been the "longest night" she's ever known.

ACT 4 SCENE 3

Eglamour arrives at Silvia's window as requested. He says he is her "servant" and her friend. She explains her situation and tells him she plans to run away to find Valentine and begs him to accompany her. He agrees to help and they arrange to meet that evening at Friar Patrick's cell.

ACT 4 SCENE 4

Lines 1–55: Lance says he was sent to make a gift of Crab to Silvia. Unfortunately Crab misbehaved, and Lance goes on to recount further examples of his misbehavior, complaining all the while of the dog's ingratitude and how he has saved him in the past from whipping and worse. Proteus arrives with Julia, still disguised as a boy, giving her name as Sebastian. Proteus says he likes him/her and will employ him. When he sees Lance, he asks him if Silvia liked the "little jewel" of a dog he sent as a gift. Lance says she refused it and he's brought the dog back again, indicating Crab. Proteus is puzzled but Lance explains that the "other squirrel" was stolen from him so he offered her his own dog instead. Proteus is furious and sends Lance off to find his dog.

Lines 56–103: Proteus asks Sebastian (Julia) to deliver a ring from him to Silvia, saying that she who gave it to him "loved me well." Julia says he can't have loved her to give it away, and suggests she may be dead. When Proteus says he doesn't think so, she cries "Alas!" and when he asks her why, she replies because she who gave him the ring must have loved him as much as he loves Silvia. It was pity that made her cry. He points out Silvia's chamber and tells her to give her the ring anyway and to remind her that she's promised to give him her picture. She is to return to him afterward. Now alone, Julia considers her situation, feeling pity for Proteus because she truly loves him. She says she will woo Silvia for him, but "coldly," since she doesn't want his suit to her to succeed.

Lines 104–174: Sebastian/Julia asks to speak to Silvia, who thinks s/he's come for the picture. As she hands it over she says to tell Proteus he would better hang a picture of Julia in his chamber. Sebastian/Julia asks her to read her master's letter, but Silvia refuses and tears it up. S/he then gives her the ring, which Silvia refuses, recognizing it as the ring given him by Julia. Sebastian/Julia thanks her and when Silvia asks why, s/he says for her care for Julia. Silvia asks if s/he knows Julia and s/he replies "Almost as well as I do know myself." Silvia asks her to describe Julia and s/he describes herself as she was. S/he says she knows they are the same size since Sebastian borrowed a gown from Julia for a pageant, in which he played a woman, a "lamentable part," the deserted Ariadne of classical mythology "passioning / For Theseus' perjury and unjust flight." S/he describes her performance, which was "so lively acted" that it made Julia weep. Silvia pities her and condemns Proteus' treatment. She gives Sebastian/Julia a purse and leaves.

Lines 175–201: Now alone, Julia reflects on Silvia and her honesty and kindness, hoping that Proteus will not succeed with her. Looking at her picture, she concludes that Silvia is no prettier than herself and tries to understand why Proteus should now prefer her. She reflects on the blindness and contrariness of love, confessing that, although she's jealous of the kisses and adoration that the picture will receive, she'll treat it kindly for Silvia's sake, otherwise she'd have scratched out the "unseeing eyes" so that Proteus would fall out of love with her image.

ACT 5 SCENE 1

Eglamour and Silvia meet at Friar Patrick's and set off for the forest.

ACT 5 SCENE 2

Turio and Proteus are discussing the progress of Turio's courtship of Silvia. Proteus gives flattering, ambiguous responses to each of

Turio's questions, while Julia, as Sebastian, is standing by offering ironic asides. The Duke arrives, asking whether they have seen Silvia recently. When they say they haven't, he realizes she's fled with Eglamour to find Valentine. They each decide to follow for different reasons.

ACT 5 SCENE 3

Silvia has been captured by the Outlaws who are going to take her to their "captain's cave."

ACT 5 SCENE 4

Lines 1–62: Valentine, alone, reflects on the peace and tranquillity he enjoys in the forest. He hears a commotion and, recognizing his fellow Outlaws, stands aside to observe events. Proteus enters with Silvia and Julia (still disguised as Sebastian). Proteus says he has rescued her from dishonor and deserves at least a kind look from her. Valentine can't believe what he's hearing. Silvia says how "miserable" and "unhappy" she is, but Proteus says she was unhappy until he came and now she should be happy. Silvia responds that his approach makes her "most unhappy." In an aside, Julia says it makes her unhappy too. Silvia says she'd rather be eaten by a lion than rescued by Proteus. She loves Valentine and detests "false perjured Proteus." She accuses him of betraying both Julia and his friend. Proteus replies that friendship doesn't count in love and since she will not be wooed by words, he'll woo her like a soldier and force her.

Lines 63–89: Valentine steps forward and orders Proteus to let her go. Proteus is shocked. Valentine says that only the evidence of his own eyes could have convinced him of Proteus' treachery and villainy. He is full of sorrow but they must be enemies from now on. Proteus says he is overcome with "shame and guilt" and truly sorry for his actions. He begs forgiveness. Valentine at once forgives him, saying he is satisfied and to prove his love for his friend, he will give up Silvia to Proteus: "All that was mine in Silvia I give thee." Still standing aside, the disguised Julia exclaims "O, me unhappy!" and faints.

Lines 90–125: Valentine asks Sebastian/Julia what the matter is and s/he says she was supposed to deliver a ring to Silvia. When Proteus asks for the ring she produces the ring he had originally given her as a keepsake when they parted. When asked how she came by it she finally reveals herself. He is surprised but Julia tells him not to be, it's a lesser evil for women to change their appearance than men their minds. He is stung by her words, and seeing Julia in front of him, cannot understand why he should have preferred Silvia. The four are reconciled and take hands, when the Outlaws enter having captured the Duke and Turio.

Lines 126–179: Valentine tells the Outlaws to let them go and welcomes the Duke. The Duke is astonished, but seeing Silvia, Turio claims her. Valentine threatens to kill him and Turio gives her up at once: "I hold him but a fool that will endanger // His body for a girl that loves him not." The Duke is disgusted by his cowardliness and admires Valentine's courageous determination, which proves in the Duke's mind that he is "a gentleman" and fit to marry his daughter. Valentine thanks him and asks one more favor—that he will pardon the Outlaws, who are now reformed, and find them employment. The Duke agrees and as they all set out to return home, Valentine promises to explain everything to him, including the "blushes" of the "page." That done they will marry and all live happily.

THE TWO GENTLEMEN OF VERONA IN PERFORMANCE: THE RSC AND BEYOND

The best way to understand a Shakespeare play is to see it or ideally to participate in it. By examining a range of productions, we may gain a sense of the extraordinary variety of approaches and interpretations that are possible—a variety that gives Shakespeare his unique capacity to be reinvented and made "our contemporary" four centuries after his death.

We begin with a brief overview of the play's theatrical and cinematic life, offering historical perspectives on how it has been performed. We then analyze in more detail a series of productions staged over the last half-century by the Royal Shakespeare Company. The sense of dialogue between productions that can only occur when a company is dedicated to the revival and investigation of the Shakespeare canon over a long period, together with the uniquely comprehensive archival resource of promptbooks, program notes, reviews, and interviews held on behalf of the RSC at the Shakespeare Birthplace Trust in Stratford-upon-Avon, allows an "RSC stage history" to become a crucible in which the chemistry of the play can be explored.

Finally, we go to the horse's mouth. Modern theater is dominated by the figure of the director, who must hold together the whole play, whereas the actor must concentrate on his or her part. The director's viewpoint is therefore especially valuable. Shakespeare's plasticity is wonderfully revealed when we hear directors of highly successful productions answering the same questions in very different ways.

FOUR CENTURIES OF *THE TWO GENTLEMEN*: AN OVERVIEW

One of the least regularly performed of Shakespeare's comedies, *The Two Gentlemen of Verona* is perhaps most familiar to modern audiences from John Madden's film *Shakespeare in Love*. In the banqueting hall at Whitehall, Judi Dench's Queen Elizabeth nods off, bored, as Henry Condell delivers Valentine's earnest soliloquy, "What light is light . . . ," and laughs uproariously as Will Kempe (Patrick Barlow) clowns with his dog as Lance. Backstage, Philip Henslowe (Geoffrey Rush) turns to Shakespeare and sums up: "Love and a bit with a dog, that's what they like."[1] The responses of Elizabeth and Henslowe are characteristic of modern expectations of the play in performance: a light entertainment, with only the Lance/Crab comic scenes and the problematic ending usually worthy of notice. Yet the relative obscurity of the play has also been found to work in the play's favor, as it retains the ability in the hands of strong companies to excite and surprise, as well as lending itself to weightier issues.

There are no recorded performances of the play until 1762 at London's Drury Lane, where David Garrick directed an adaptation by Benjamin Victor. Victor prefaced the published version thus:

> It is the general opinion, that this comedy abounds with weeds; and there is no one, I think, will deny, who peruses it with attention, that it is adorned with several poetical flowers, such as the hand of a Shakespeare alone could raise. The rankest of those weeds I have endeavoured to remove; but was not a little solicitous lest I should go too far, and, while I fancy'd myself grubbing up a weed, should heedlessly cut the threads of a flower.[2]

The most significant of the "weeds" was Valentine's "gift" of Silvia to Proteus in the play's final scene, an act too unconscionable for the sentimental eighteenth-century stage. The cutting of this moment in order to soften the play's darker edges was still practiced well into the twentieth century. In Victor's version, Valentine admonishes Proteus and claims Silvia unreservedly for himself:

> Kind heav'n has heard my fervent prayer!
> And brought my faithful Silvia to my arms!
> There is no rhetoric can express my joy![3]

The renewal of the two men's friendship follows the reunion of Proteus and Julia, prioritizing marriage over male homosocial bonds. There is also a good deal of added business for Lance and Crab, including a prisoner trick that recalls the deception of Parolles in *All's Well That Ends Well*.

A text closer to Shakespeare's was produced at Covent Garden in 1784, but was not revived after its first performance. It was perhaps most notable for John Quick, as Lance, delivering an address following the main performance "riding on an elephant."[4] John Philip Kemble's staging at Drury Lane in 1790 managed three performances, and was noted for a serenade in the fourth act performed by Charles Dignum. Kemble himself went on to play one of the oldest Valentines in the play's performance history at Covent Garden in 1808, at the age of fifty.

In 1821, Frederick Reynolds initiated an influential tradition of turning the play into an opera in a successful production at Covent Garden. The *European Magazine* reported:

> In the fourth [act], the Carnival was displayed in more than its customary glories. The opening of the scene displayed the Ducal Palace and great square of Milan illuminated, golden gondolas on the river, and all the usual appendages of foreign gala, masquers, dancing girls, and mountebanks.[5]

The opera was praised for its grand spectacle and pageantry, including processions of the seasons and elements, and the appearance of Cleopatra's galley; and the performances, including Jones' spirited Valentine, were applauded. It was criticized, however, for being lengthy and overcrowded with songs. It set a precedent for later musical adaptations of the play, including Augustin Daly's 1895 "vaudeville" version,[6] Mel Shapiro's 1971 rock musical, and the BBC film's use of period madrigals.

William Charles Macready used a more straightforward text for his 1841 production at Drury Lane, including the restoration of Valentine's offer of Silvia, played in a whirl of emotional excess at the play's conclusion. Interestingly, although Lance received his share of the notices, Miss Fortescue's Julia commanded the most applause:

In the single character of Julia, Shakespeare may be said at once to have reached perfection, for throughout his works we shall not find a personage more beautifully conceived or more delicately organized . . . The maidenlike unwillingness to discover her passion even in the presence of an attendant, who is almost a confidant; the rapture with which she owns her love to herself when free from a witness; the feminine vanity which allows her to contrast herself favourably with Sylvia . . . all these traits are so many threads to draw down a character from the regions of abstractions.[7]

In Julia, the Victorian stage found its ideal heroine. Macready's promptbook formed the basis of Charles Kean's mounting, which toured America and returned to London's Haymarket in 1848. The review in *The Times* summed up the preexisting bias against the play that would continue to dominate critical responses:

The meagreness of the story, the absence of effective situations, and the crudity of construction, will always prevent this play from being a permanent favourite with the public, in spite of the poetical beauties and genuine comic humour with which it abounds.[8]

It was again Julia who most caught the attention of reviewers, this time played by Ellen Tree: "Her by-play in the scene when Proteus serenades Sylvia, and when she scrutinizes every face till she has discovered that of her faithless lover, and then bursts into a mute agony of grief, is one of the best things she has done."[9] The other significant production of this era was that of Samuel Phelps at Sadler's Wells in 1857, about which unfortunately little is known.

Augustin Daly's production played in New York and London in early 1895, and was savaged by Bernard Shaw who objected to Daly's cutting of the more poetical passages in preference for functional exposition, and complained:

All through the drama the most horribly common music repeatedly breaks out on the slightest pretext or on no pretext at all . . . Mr. Worthing [Valentine] charged himself with feeling without any particular reference to his lines; and Mr. Craig [Proteus] struck a balance by attending to the meaning of his speeches without taking them at all to heart.[10]

Shaw did, however, reserve a qualified note of praise for Lance and Crab, whose scenes "brought out the latent silliness and childishness of the audience as Shakespear's [sic] clowning scenes always do: I laugh at them like a yokel myself," and for Ada Rehan's Julia who "stirred some feeling into the part" as well as providing "a strong argument for rational dress by looking much better in her page's costume than in that of her own sex."[11] In New York, Julia was once more a star role, "but not even Miss Rehan's pleasing exhibition of herself in page-boy costume, nor the moonlit lake Daly invented for the environs of Milan, nor a thunderstorm in the final act could make up for the tenuousness of the narrative."[12]

Preconceptions about the quality of the play, often excused as juvenilia and a forerunner to worthier comedies, continued to influence twentieth-century reviewers; *The Times* noted of Ben Iden Payne's 1938 Stratford Memorial Theatre production, "All the chief romantic characters are continually vexed by the ghosts of their descendants,"[13] though there were exceptions. William Poel staged the play at His Majesty's Theatre in London for Herbert Beerbohm Tree in 1910, following earlier productions in the 1890s. Beerbohm Tree, famous for his Victorian spectaculars, was diametrically opposed to Poel's Elizabethan-influenced, bare-stage approach, but allowed Poel to build out an apron stage over the orchestra pit to his own specifications. As a result, "the literary quality of the play, the verve of its dialogue, the lyric beauty of many of its passages came out with unusual freshness and clear-cut relief."[14]

As it did not afford an obvious starring role for the great actor-managers, the play was rarely performed or reviewed during their heyday. In 1904, Harley Granville-Barker took the role of Speed at the Royal Court, while Frank Benson played the First Outlaw in his mounting at the Shakespeare Memorial Theatre in 1910. At this stage, the play was primarily treated as a curio that needed to be "resolved"—J. C. Trewin noted that Granville-Barker's production

Julia (Ada Rehan)

1. Augustin Daly's 1896–97 New York production with Ada Rehan as Julia who "stirred some feeling into the part" as well as providing "a strong argument for rational dress by looking much better in her page's costume than in that of her own sex."

"was smoothed along gracefully,"[15] while Benson's succeeded "in spite of its maddening ending," which continued to cause problems for reviewers wanting neat sentiments.[16] In 1925, meanwhile, one reviewer generously called William Bridges-Adams' mounting

> A fresh and successful experiment. Although it is light in struc-
> ture and has no great acting part, it is surprising that it should
> so seldom be performed for it is a melodious play, full of witty
> contrivance and written in a verse that sings.[17]

The Stratford performance history of the play is unremarkable, although Ben Greet's 1916 production did feature Sybil Thorndike as Julia, and Paddy Rainbow made an impression as Crab. The Crab/Lance scenes remained the chief draw, as in Payne's production:

> So far as individual performances go it is Mr. Jay Laurier's
> evening. This comedian finds in Launce a character almost
> perfectly suited to his humour, and whenever he is on the stage
> we are in contact with something that is more than a mere
> foreshadowing of greater things to come.[18]

Denis Carey's exuberant production by a young cast for the Bristol Old Vic in 1952 was broadcast on BBC1, ironing over the more prob-lematic areas of the play with a zestful approach. Muriel St. Clare Byrne contrasted it with Michael Langham's important 1956 pro-duction at London's Old Vic. Set in a Regency era of Byronic heroes and décor reminiscent of Jane Austen:

> The sentiments and the clothes go perfectly together. There is
> an essential frivolity about Regency costume which persuades
> us to abandon our disapproval of Proteus and our concern for
> the ladies' feelings as irrelevant. If the producer can make us
> agree to accept it as artificial comedy, set in an age where we
> take romantic absurdity for granted, he can restore to the play
> a gaiety with which I believe its author tried to endow it.[19]

2. Ben Iden Payne's 1938 production for the Stratford Memorial Theatre: Lance and Pantino. While "all the chief romantic characters are continually vexed by the ghosts of their descendants," Jay Laurier (left) "finds in Launce a character almost perfectly suited to his humour, and whenever he is on the stage we are in contact with something that is more than a mere foreshadowing of greater things to come."

In this world of emotional excesses, the ending came as a perfect climax of sensibility and swooning, in which a repentant Proteus threatened to kill himself with a pistol, prompting Valentine's offer of Silvia. Langham's production reintroduced *Two Gentlemen* to the repertory as a play of some merit.

The play has rarely been filmed, but Don Taylor's gentle studio production for the BBC/Time Life series in 1983 drew on Botticelli for a poetic, faithful presentation that used a formal garden setting and towers to exaggerate the play's lyricism. There have been several foreign language screen adaptations, including *Yī jiǎn méi* (*A Spray of Plum Blossoms*), a silent Chinese film from 1931, and the 1964 German TV version *Die zwei herren aus Verona*. More effective in reaching a large audience was Mel Shapiro's Tony Award–winning rock musical of 1971, playing to appreciative crowds on Broadway and in the West End. Featuring numbers such as "Night Letter" and the climactic "Love Has Driven Me Sane," the multiracial cast and provocative score captured a zeitgeist alongside shows such as *Hair* and *Grease*, introducing the story to a new generation of theatergoers.

Two noteworthy productions were staged at Stratford, Ontario. Robin Phillips directed a faithful 1975 version set on the Italian Riviera. Most notable was a reversal of the usual Valentine/Proteus dynamic:

Stephen Russell . . . presented a dangerously volatile, restlessly physical Valentine who worked out with boxing gloves, threw a beach ball about, and displayed all the attributes of his type: frankness, generosity, impulsiveness, and a shortage of acumen. Nicholas Pennell played the softer Proteus as a young man not devious by nature but grasping at duplicity as the only weapon that might serve him against such as Valentine in his pursuit of Silvia. He came to contrition at the end in the same way that Valentine abandoned his anger, almost with relief.[20]

Jackie Burrough's forthright Silvia was also praised: "You felt she was enjoying herself, and that the touch of chagrin in her silence following Valentine's intervention was as much the result of being prevented from dealing with Proteus in her own way as of finding her-self, for once, not the center of attention."[21] In 1984, Leon Rubin directed the Young Company at the Third Stage in a New Wave–inflected production where an uproarious Crab upstaged a weak Lance, but in which the complexities of Proteus were finely drawn:

> [David Clark] plays Proteus as an ebullient undergraduate whose apparently harmless self-absorption turns vicious and proves ultimately as painful to him as it has to others . . . He becomes so plausible an opportunist that he makes easy game of Valentine . . . and so ardent a spokesman of the poetry of courtship that he justly holds Milan and Thurio spellbound at his recital.[22]

In the UK, Jeremy James Taylor set his Young Vic production in a formal French garden that "manages, in fact, to reconcile two different approaches: hand-on-heart and tongue-in-cheek."[23] The women were stately in public but prone to giggles and irreverence when private and, unusually, Peter O'Farrell's Turio was singled out for praise, "whirring around the Junoesque Sylvia (Joanna McCallum) with incredible speed and holding balletic postures like a vainglorious white mouse."[24]

Charles Newell's 1990 American touring production with the Acting Company marked a growing interest in self-conscious theatricality, opening to the sound of an orchestra tuning up and two projected silhouettes of Valentine and Proteus struggling over a baton. To a score of freeform jazz, the play spiraled toward its chaotic climax:

> The attempted rape of Silvia is horrifyingly realistic. She and Proteus overturn a couch in a struggle that lasts several min-utes, and, when she resists, he slaps her viciously. This rapist means business. Valentine's intervention is equally brutal—he only just resists bringing a log down on his betrayer's skull with killing force. The image visually echoes their opening wrestling bout.[25]

The notion that the play's value was to be found in its darker edges would gain increasing currency in the twenty-first century.

In 1996, the reconstructed Globe in London opened with Jack Shepherd's production of *Two Gentlemen*, with Mark Rylance as Proteus and Anastasia Hille as Silvia. Most reviewers were more concerned with the new space, which had a significant impact on the performance: for example, audience members hissed at Proteus' plans. Rylance, "although peddling a sharp comic line in repressed, buttoned-up gaucheness, is a sentimental study of the villain as little boy lost."[26] Three years later, Julia Anne Robinson directed the play in the Cottesloe at London's National Theatre, a production received well by its intended school audiences.

As with *The Merchant of Venice* and *The Two Noble Kinsmen*, the central male friendship of *Two Gentlemen* can be usefully appropriated for a more explicitly homosexual reading. Stuart Draper's 2004 production transferred from New York to London, and announced its intentions in a prologue where,

> To the dying strains of an orchestral regurgitation of the Bee Gees' hit "Tragedy," the two Veronese gentlemen begin canoodling under a tree. As Valentine finishes reciting Christopher Marlowe's amorous lyric "Come live with me and be my love" to his boyfriend Proteus, the latter's father steams in and begins shouting abuse while Valentine is taken to one side and duffed up by his henchmen.[27]

Performed in a spirit of "raucous caricature and high camp,"[28] this energetic version found a new narrative for the comedy with serious, unsettling undertones concerning prejudice and familial expectations.

While a return by theater companies to the ironic use of farce has been enlightening in the case of some of Shakespeare's early comedies (particularly *The Comedy of Errors* and *The Taming of the Shrew*), in the case of *Two Gentlemen* the play itself risks being lost under its parodic adaptations (such as a *Dawson's Creek* TV episode entitled "Two Gentlemen of Capeside" [2000]; Adam Bertocci's hysterical amalgamation of Shakespeare and the Coen Brothers in

Two Gentlemen of Lebowski, 2009).[29] However, the use of physical comedy and playful theatricality has, in different cultural contexts, recently offered fresh perspectives on the play, as in Helena Pimenta's production for the Basque ur Teatro, which used a hedonistic 1920s music hall style to critique the evasion of moral responsibility. In 2006, the Brazilian company Nós do Morro ("Us From the Hillside," a group from Vidigal, a shantytown outside Río de Janeiro) visited the RSC Complete Works Festival in partnership with the Birmingham youth project Gallery 37 (a talented group of underprivileged young people from Birmingham), in a production that adapted the play to the concerns of council estates and favela (Brazilian shantytown) life. The English children wrote their own rap music, which they performed as a group Chorus, mediating the plot and using their bodies to create scenery on a bare stage. The Brazilian actors, meanwhile, used a Portuguese text to turn the play into a series of lyrical combats, with one memorable sequence involving Valentine and Turio performing a "sing-off" in a makeshift boxing ring. The play belonged to Diogo de Brito Sales, however, as a human Crab who bounded among the audience, pretending to lick faces.

Similarly left field was Two Gents' Productions' *Vakomana Vaviri Ve Zimbabwe*. This international two-man touring production, performed in the style of Zimbabwean township theater, was lively and informal, filled with audience participation. Simple items of clothing (a glove for Silvia; braces for Valentine) signified characters, with Tonderai Munyevu and Denton Chikura acting as storytellers—a character could literally be passed between the two. Julia visited a witch doctor in order to see a vision of Proteus wooing Silvia; and Crab was once more played by a human, though his bitter disdain of Lance had an edge to it. The frenetic comedy, however, gave way to a powerful closing image. Proteus and Valentine had reunited, while Julia and Silvia "lay" on the floor as discarded garments. While the men's reunion was joyous, the women were visibly forgotten. As the lights faded to black and the two actors once more became the women. Julia moved to the sobbing Silvia, taking her head in her lap. In these stripped-back productions, *The Two Gentlemen of Verona* transcended its trivial reputation, and its translation into fresh cultural contexts continues to unlock fresh potential in this neglected play.

AT THE RSC

The Two Gentlemen of Verona is an early Shakespeare play—perhaps the earliest. It is often argued that its main interest lies in a first glimpse of characters, conventions, and tropes which Shakespeare develops and deploys more successfully in later work:

> In innumerable ways *Two Gentlemen of Verona* looks forward to Shakespeare's later comedies. The character of Julia and her masculine disguise, the central position of the women in the play, the serious use of the clowns as commentators, and of music, themes of travel, and the transformation of people through love, the greenwood as the place where pretences are dropped and characters appear for what they really are, the carefully calculated mixture of prose and verse, all of these motifs and devices were to be extended and developed in succeeding plays. Yet the *Two Gentlemen* has a freshness and lyrical charm all its own, an uncertain glory that is no more to be despised than that of the April day described by Proteus, wavering between brilliance and cloud.[30]

Times and Spaces

In 1960 in the newly refurbished Shakespeare Memorial Theatre (soon to be renamed the Royal Shakespeare Theatre) Peter Hall directed a sequence of six Shakespearean comedies suggesting in the program notes that "the early romantic comedy, *The Two Gentlemen of Verona*, first reveals Shakespeare's flair for mixing romance, realism, lyricism and clowning. This matures in *The Merchant of Venice* and is at its best in *Twelfth Night*. But in each of these three plays there is a dark side that almost spoils the fun."

It was set in "that 'ingenious Italy,' rich in storytelling and the land of lyric love." Renzo Mongiardino's sets and Lila de Nobili's Renaissance costumes looked lovely, but overall the production was not judged a success, due in large part to problems with the set, as described by A. Alvarez:

> The theatre now has a revolving stage, an apron jutting into the stalls and a new resident director. The opening production of *The Two Gentlemen of Verona* seemed designed chiefly to show off these assets. The stage twirled so constantly and fast that it seemed at times more like *Carousel* than Shakespeare; the leading characters each took their turn on the apron stage, trying to break down the fourth wall and buttonhole the audience; and Peter Hall tried nearly every trick in the book to relieve the monotony of very early Shakespeare. But it's heavy going: the plot and development are conventional and the verse monotonous. Yet I'm not at all sure that the play's longueurs are as inevitable as he makes them seem.[31]

Despite Hall's many "advantages as a Shakespearean director," understanding of the play and "respect for the language as poetry" and the ability "to force a high standard of verse-speaking on his cast," Alvarez claimed that

> he has a vice: he is a sucker for a pretty scene; and in Renzo Mongiardino he has a designer all too able to pander to him. The stage was so littered with ivied ruins and bits of decaying gilded interiors that it looked like an opulent, tinted Piranesi. Pretty enough in itself . . . yet it contrived to make an immature play seem altogether decadent.[32]

Subsequent productions have eschewed attempts at Renaissance picturesqueness, locating the play in twentieth-century sets and costumes, seeking modern resonances for the play's *jejeune* qualities. For Robin Phillips' 1970 production, the Royal Shakespeare Theatre was updated to a 1960s lido with beachwear, sunglasses, and onstage swimming pool. Daphne Dare's set consisted of "a ramp and steps from mid-stage left and a small pool downstage right. The forest was created by the dropping of a single batten of ropes from the flies and a dappling of the light."[33] The play opened with a recording of "Who

3. Peter Hall's 1960 production with Lucetta (Mavis Edwards, behind) teasing Julia (Frances Cuka) about her letter, Act 1 Scene 2: "The stage was so littered with ivied ruins and bits of decaying gilded interiors that it looked like an opulent, tinted Piranesi . . . it contrived to make an immature play seem altogether decadent."

is Sylvia? Who is Valentine? Who is Proteus? Who is Julia?" and closed with the Beatles' "All You Need Is Love." B. A. Young argued that the choice of setting was logical: "Courts being out of fashion in the 20th century, Mr Phillips has sent his young people to a Milanese university where their behaviour fits in very suitably."[34] Gareth Lloyd Evans believed that "for all the many visual and thematic inconsistencies induced by such a treatment, it seemed to me to have been done in a spirit of affection rather than disdain of this immature play."[35]

John Barton's 1981 production paired Shakespeare's earliest comedy with his earliest tragedy in a double bill with *Titus Andronicus*. It was a brave experiment that employed a conscious metatheatricality in its cross-casting and onstage audience. Both plays were severely cut—850 lines from *Titus* and 515 from *Two Gentlemen*. It confused and divided critics. Roger Warren was the most perceptive in his understanding of how the two plays worked together:

Mr Barton's interpretation of *The Two Gentlemen of Verona* must be considered in relation to his treatment of *Titus Andronicus*, which preceded it in a double-bill at Stratford.

The acting area was reduced to a very confined space at the front of the stage, surrounded by racks containing costumes, weapons, and props, and by the hobby-horses used by the Goths in *Titus* and by Silvia, Eglamour and Thurio in their flight to the forest in *Two Gentlemen*. Patrick Stewart (Titus) announced the play's title and read the opening stage directions. The actors visibly assumed their characterizations before entries and switched them off again once they were out of the acting area; they watched scenes they were not in, and often provided sound effects, such as birdsong for the various forest scenes. Perhaps surprisingly, this artifice did not on the whole rob the events of conviction. Sometimes the actors' presence distracted, as when the actress playing young Lucius had her hair dressed at a central prop table; but more often it led into scenes, as when Saturninus watched the Andronici shooting arrows into his court before storming on to complain "what

wrongs are these," or made interesting connections between
episodes, as when the watching Julia laughed in sympathetic
recognition at Valentine's confusion over the love-letter Silvia
had asked him to write: it was as if, like Touchstone, she was
thinking that "we that are true lovers run into strange capers."[36]

4. John Barton's 1981 RSC production was played in a double bill with *Titus
Andronicus*. "The actors visibly assumed their characterizations before
entries and switched them off again once they were out of the acting area;
they watched scenes they were not in . . . [making] interesting connections
between episodes, as when the watching Julia laughed in sympathetic
recognition at Valentine's confusion over the love-letter Silvia had asked
him to write" (Act 2 Scene 1) with Julia Swift (Julia) overlooking Diana Hard-
castle (Silvia) and Peter Chelsom (Valentine).

Critics, dismayed by the ruthless treatment of the text in Barton's production, were delighted by David Thacker's far more cavalier approach, which in the event was so successful from its opening in April 1991 that it toured and was revived (with minor cast changes) until the end of 1993. Rex Gibson argues that it was

> a brilliant demonstration of Noel Coward's adage: "Never underestimate the power of cheap music." Thacker backs the action of Shakespeare's wonderfully unrealistic romance with a 1930s Café de Paris band. The musicians, with centre-parted, sleeked-down hair, immaculate in evening dress, embody the tacky sophistication of love songs with which their platinum blonde singer punctuates each scene. "Blue Moon," "Night and Day," and most tellingly, "Love is the Sweetest Thing" superbly underscore the improbable events of the play.[37]

Margaret Ingram's account conveys an authentic sense of the audience's response to this infectious production that also explains its popularity:

> No-one has ever been more aware than Shakespeare that music is a necessary accompaniment to love; is, indeed, its food, as Orsino proclaims at the beginning of *Twelfth Night*, begging excess of it that his appetite might be sated. Nothing has changed in 400 years, except that in this production of what was probably Shakespeare's first tentative play about love and betrayal, director David Thacker has had the wit to turn this excess into music so much of our own time that there was hardly a member of the audience who was not responding emotively to *The Two Gentlemen of Verona* with their own pleasurable memories of the music and song that has been around with never decreasing popularity since the 30s.
>
> [That] they were meant to be in the mood for enjoyment long before the action started was made clear by the beckoning of the ushers to the throng around the bars with the news that the music had begun and we would surely be sorry to miss it.

Wonderingly, therefore, we took our seats to the sound of a Cole Porter lyric delightfully sung by Hilary Crome, accompanied by what was surely the Palm Court Orchestra playing at the back of the stage framed in spring blossom but so invitingly empty that it was a wonder no-one sprang on to it and danced. For surely we had been invited to a ball? Perhaps not; but that was the feeling induced and the happiness of the evening was thus successfully radiated before the play began.

This musical accompaniment continued enjoyably throughout every scene change and necessary piece of business while the stage was transformed from Verona to Milan and trimly filled with 30s furniture, tennis gear, cabin trunks, sunshine and bright young things in 30s dress. The songs underlined in their own way the love, betrayal and infidelity of human nature and the frailty of youth's protestations and promises. Snatches of *Love's Own Sweet Song*, *Heartache*, *Love in Bloom* and *The Glory of Love* filled in the message.[38]

Thacker's was a hard act to follow. Edward Hall's 1998 production, also in the Swan Theatre, offered more "bright young things" in an up-to-the-minute Italian take on the play, which Russell Jackson described as "*La Dolce Vita*, ca. 1998, rather than *Cavalleria Rusticana*, 1910." It was a busy production with lots of noise, parties, designer chic, and supernumeraries for doormen, bellboys, and whores, as Jackson went on to elaborate:

Hall found room for plenty of sharp ideas, some of which established milieu deftly: a gangplank and pre-voyage drinks to send Proteus off to Milan; a bar revealed by folding back the louvered shutters on one side of the back wall; traffic noise and oncoming headlights evoked the outskirts of the city where Valentine meets the bandits; a desolate place for the final scene.[39]

Fiona Buffini's 2004 production toured in repertory with *Julius Caesar* (not in a double bill though). Michael Billington related the setting to Thacker's earlier production:

Like David Thacker a decade ago, Fiona Buffini has set *Two Gents* in the 1930s. But where Thacker beguiled us with pop songs by Gershwin and Porter, Buffini uses the period setting to bring out the high style of Milan, which becomes a fashion-plate whirl of slinky women, brilliantined men, hectic parties and hot jazz.[40]

Patricia Tatspaugh described it as

Set between the wars, with a successful blending of design and direction, Fiona Buffini's *Two Gentlemen of Verona* for the RSC's small-scale tour depicted an autumnal Verona inhabited by English gentry in decline and Milan as the sophisticated social capital of the jazz age.[41]

It is perhaps a reflection of its relatively humble place in the Shakespearean canon that *The Two Gentlemen of Verona* enjoyed the

5. Fiona Buffini's 2004 RSC production in the Swan Theatre with Alex Avery (Valentine), Rachel Pickup (Silvia), and Zubin Varla as Turio: Milan became "a fashion-plate whirl of slinky women, brilliantined men, hectic parties and hot jazz."

smallest number of performances of any play within the RSC's Complete Works Festival with a single performance on 27 August 2006 at the Courtyard Theatre. Guti Fraga directed a lively, colorful production in English and Portuguese, which combined the talents of Nós do Morro and Gallery 37.

Twoness and Twosomes

The program notes to Edward Hall's 1998 production argue that "The title of *The Two Gentlemen of Verona* proclaims the play's thematic interest in 'twoness' and its insistence upon the concept of a sense of proper behavior. An intrinsic duality informs the structural pattern." This is manifested in the two pairs of lovers, two fathers, two comic servants, two rival suitors, even, although we never see Proteus' "little jewel" (4.4.42), two dogs. A production works dramatically by contrasts and distinctions but must nevertheless find a convincing way to achieve the unity promised in the play's conclusion, "One feast, one house, one mutual happiness."

The two gentlemen have the largest but also the most problematic parts (Proteus 20 percent and Valentine 17 percent). In 1960 Derek Godfrey's "handsomely Italianate" Proteus was perhaps too well contrasted with Denholm Elliott's Valentine in a shoulder-length blond wig, "one subtly experienced and the other innocent, solves at a glance any problems raised by their vulnerable friendship. Mr Elliott, indeed, is almost too benevolent, not far from Aguecheek in simplicity [*Twelfth Night*]. In fact his kindly personality makes the robbers' choice of him as their leader more than usually incredible."[42] The trickiest moment comes when, having attempted to rape Silvia, Proteus is nevertheless forgiven and offered "All that was mine in Silvia" (5.4.88) by Valentine. John Russell Brown describes this moment in Hall's production as "spoken so that it was hardly noticed; Proteus' repentance was a sentiment to laugh at."[43]

Robin Phillips' production (with Ian Richardson as Proteus and Peter Egan as Valentine) attempted to suggest plausible psychological reasons for Proteus' conduct:

As Ian Richardson plays him, it is clear that his shortness compared both to Valentine and Thurio, whose lithe beachboy figure he enviously paws, is a source of lack of confidence. His double-dealing of both men is therefore motivated here not so much by the requirements of a plot borrowed from literary sources but by the spiteful jealousy of a confused adolescent. Thus when this friend and lover with all his hang-ups is paid the ultimate compliment of being offered his best friend's mistress at the close of play, this previously unplayable scene can be said to offer some meaning in the light of current recherché theories of displaced homosexuality.[44]

Helen Mirren's Julia, "a blonde-wigged tigress,"[45] drew considerable critical comment (mostly favorable): "Helen Mirren . . . brings the only emotional force to the evening. Her acting shows extraordinary truth and strength."[46] There was praise also for minor roles: "Sebastian Shaw's wonderfully funny Scoutmaster Sir Eglamour is as solemn in realisation as it is comic in conception. Clement McCallin has made the Duke laughable by giving a straight performance and a very good one, of a figure who simply doesn't belong in those surroundings."[47] Harold Hobson concluded that the production,

By way of beachwear and the Lido . . . reaches the heart of Shakespeare's play—the rapture of its youth and the darkness of its treachery—and finds it beating fresh and strong. It treats with masterly nonchalance the more absurd parts of the story, but where the verse is great, it is greatly spoken. Whether grave or playful, Mr Phillips' touch is unfaltering, to the play's essence totally loyal.[48]

John Barton's production had its own version of "twoness" playing in a double bill with *Titus Andronicus*. Patrick Stewart (Lance in the 1970 *Two Gents*, see below) played Titus and Sheila Hancock, Tamora. As the leads in the earlier play, it was they who, despite taking minor roles in *Two Gents*, claimed most critical attention. Stewart played Sir Eglamour and Sheila Hancock the leader of the Outlaws:

After the interval, she [Hancock] bounded cheerfully forward to announce *Two Gentlemen*. The sheer contrast with *Titus* was

6. Robin Phillips' 1970 RSC production with Helen Mirren as Julia (here in disguise as the page, Sebastian) and Ian Richardson as Proteus: Mirren was described as "a blonde-wigged tigress" whose "acting shows extraordinary truth and strength" while Richardson's Proteus was motivated by "the spiteful jealousy of a confused adolescent."

bound to emphasize its humorous potential, but in addition the scenes involving Eglamour and the Outlaws were able to make humorous allusions to the treatment of *Titus* earlier on. The Outlaws were without question the funniest I have ever seen, appearing in Lincoln green hoods among the prop trees from the *Titus* forest accompanied by twittering birdsong. There were nine of them and the lines were redistributed so that the actor of Aaron [Hugh Quarshie] could call abduction and murder "petty crimes," and so that Sheila Hancock could give an astonishing performance as their leader: it was she who had stabbed a gentleman "in my mood"; she immediately fell for Valentine, praising him as "a *linguist!*" in tones of rapt admiration, and later telling Silvia with evident disappointment that Valentine would "not use a woman lawlessly." She was also armed with a blunderbuss which suddenly went off, provoking an explosion of squawking from a host of "offstage" birds. The actors themselves could hardly keep straight faces after this, entirely pardonably: it was an irresistible climax to a marvellously funny scene, perfectly appropriate to Shakespeare's burlesque of Robin Hood outlaws. The treatment of Sir Eglamour was even more appropriate. Patrick Stewart's armour and gentlemanly manner recalled his Titus; with his lance, fluttering pennant, and hobby-horse he was the perfect image of an ageing knight errant, a White Knight or Don Quixote; in the forest he took on all the Outlaws at once, and since there were so many of them the textual problem of Silvia's chivalrous escort taking to his heels ceased to exist.[49]

Stanley Wells found the production "modest, charming, and sensitive to the play's weaknesses":

The gentlemen, for once, seem really young, so are more easily forgiven. Peter Land plays an initially soppy Proteus, but finds a way to convey shame and bewilderment at the unexpected shift in his emotions. Peter Chelsom's engaging Valentine, full of boyish charm and innocence, youthfully pleased with himself, has the right mixture of comedy and romance, and develops into the most interesting character. The moment of his banishment, when he kneels to John Franklin-Robbins's entertaining, strongly characterized Emperor, introduces a new dimension of seriousness; in the final scene, the genuineness of his concern both for Silvia and Proteus carries us surprisingly well through the notoriously difficult dénouement.[50]

Thacker's production also lent a comprehensible social context to the young men's behavior in the 1930s "salon society":

There is a logic to this idiom which emerges clearly on through the horseplay of the two suitors. They are public school types whose relationship, if not overtly sexual, has a competitive closeness. Schoolboy rough-and-tumble lingers on the brink of adult eroticism; a boy's own complicity is almost confusable with declarations of love.[51]

Benedict Nightingale suggests why updated versions of the play should have worked so well:

When lovers appear in doublet and hose, we expect them to behave in conventional romantic ways. Transpose them to places we can more easily associate with youthful skittishness and folly, and they can do things offensive to earnest scholars and yet seem perfectly plausible. Who knows, maybe Shakespeare meant to make romance look silly. Maybe to take liberties with this play is to be truly faithful to it. After all, every era is familiar with Proteus, the young blood who swears eternal love to one woman, then falls for his chum Valentine's girl, and proceeds to behave outrageously to everybody. At Stratford, Barry Lynch is certainly the kind of intense, secret boy who, with a little sophistry, can convince himself that his feelings are morally paramount. The last scene, with its hurried reconciliations, admittedly poses special difficulties for him, since Proteus must switch from a rapist to a penitent, in what good taste should prevent me calling a flash. Yet among men of a certain age is that really so unlikely? By then the zest and humour of Thacker's production have anyway swept away most objections.[52]

Peter Holland offered a more complex, detailed account of the play's most difficult moment:

All problems in the play pale into insignificance beside Valentine's handing over of the nearly raped Silvia to the rapist: "All that was mine in Silvia I give thee" (5.4.83). Thacker's production, while not making the line unproblematic, offered it as a problem squarely confronted and tentatively solved. The production had, slowly and thoughtfully, allowed the significance of the women to grow as the play progressed, accepting their rights to decide what happens to them, their ability to initiate action and to actualise a form of friendship that the men talk of but cannot carry through into action. It seemed only logical and fully justifiable therefore to see Silvia resolving the play's crux . . . Thacker's modest and highly intelligent solution reintegrated the moment into the development of the comedy as this production had explored it. After Proteus's "My shame and guilt confounds me" [5.4.77] Barry Lynch left a colossal pause, showing Proteus considering the possibility of conning Valentine again, before finally resolving on genuine repentance. If the audience hesitated slightly as to the genuineness of the repentance—and Lynch's smirk was so beguiling that one had to have a moment's pause—it was Silvia's silent intercession, a calm gesture of moving towards Proteus, that reassured them. Her judgement that this man was worth forgiveness justified Valentine's generosity, a symbolic act of love and respect for Silvia as much as of friendship for Proteus. Such work, accepting the play's difficulty, was as honest and intelligent as one could wish for.[53]

Robert Smallwood describes how, in Edward Hall's production,

The journey of the play was marked by two single gender, nonsexual embraces: at the end of the first scene by a valedictory hug of separation, expected all through the scene, between the leading men, Proteus and Valentine; at the end of the last scene, by an embrace of welcome and union, expected all through the scene, between the leading women, Julia and Sylvia. The embraces framed the intervening account of the awkwardnesses and inadequacies of the play's heterosexual relationships.[54]

Alastair Macaulay analyzed the leading performances perceptively, again highlighting their youth:

Four little-known young actors are given important breaks in the leading roles. Of these, the most completely successful is Poppy Miller as Silvia, who brings bite, freshness, interest to every least episode she is given. As Proteus, Dominic Rowan starts coolly but well, and with charm; later, when losing his cool, he becomes somewhat too emphatic to convince. Tom Goodman-Hill develops the opposite way as Valentine: beginning rather stiff and tepid, he acquires, when in adversity, a wonderful stillness and quiet philosophical authority that helps to explain the emotional wisdom with which he resolves the play's climax—forgiving Proteus and even offering to give up Silvia—with such brisk simplicity. Lesley Vickerage, though lacking edge, is a Julia of beauty and vulnerability.[55]

Of Fiona Buffini's 2004 production, Michael Billington argued that,

Without overplaying the point, Buffini also suggests that there is a homoerotic twist to this tale of love and betrayal in which the caddish Proteus attempts to steal his best friend's girl. When Laurence Mitchell's Proteus and Alex Avery's Valentine initially part, you half expect them to indulge in a farewell kiss. And later, when Valentine shockingly says to Proteus "All that was mine in Silvia I give thee," you realise this is a world in which male bonding counts for more than hetero urges. What is usually seen as a trial run for the later comedies here becomes an intriguing study of what Rene Girard called "triangular desire," in which two men are indissolubly linked by their desire to possess the same woman. Buffini implies all this with grace and wit. And, even if she strangely bungles the classic scene in which the eloping Valentine is caught with a tell-tale rope ladder, she brings out the extent to which the women become bemused spectators of laddish love-games. Rachel Pickup's excellent Silvia has a touching vulnerability as she is cast adrift wearing little more than a Freudian slip and Vanessa Ackerman movingly suggests that Julia's passion for Proteus is sadly misplaced.[56]

One Man and His Dog

However much or little critics enjoy the performances of the two pairs of lovers, though, it must be said that there is one double-act that never fails to delight. Shakespeare's plays are often recalled in the popular imagination by some special character, for example the ghost in *Hamlet* or the Witches in *Macbeth*. *The Two Gentlemen* has a dog. The play's two comedians Speed and Lance/Launce are admirably contrasted. Speed, as his name implies, is all quick wit and mercurial dash, and actors have generally made the most of their opportunity with the role, while Lance's fidelity to his dog provides a counterpoint to the inconsistencies of the human affections in the play.

Lance and Crab were the most widely praised performances in Peter Hall's production:

> Patrick Wymark as Launce animated his repetitive speeches by a variety of timing and emphasis, and based all on a sympathetic understanding of the large-minded, stubborn character who is yet at the mercy of circumstance. He made the audience wait for words, when he could do so without slowing up his performance, and so invited them to enter his view of the world of the play: correcting Speed for counting "slow of speech" among his maid's vices, he then looked in blank wonder at the audience so that the following line, "To be slow in words is a woman's only virtue," was the necessary statement they had been waiting for, an exaggeration which satisfied where it might have fallen dead with its stale wit.[57]

> His dog, Crab, took to the stage like a veteran. A small white terrier . . . he has the priceless theatrical attribute of repose and an uncanny knack of putting on the right expression—even a yawn . . . Most people, I think, will say they have seen a play about a dog.[58]

Patrick Stewart playing Lance in 1970 gave a richly characterized performance:

but what makes his [Phillips'] production unforgettable is his amazing vision of Launce (Patrick Stewart) and his dog, Crab. Who would have thought that this servant, usually so crude and vulgar, could so certainly be the play's sad, dark angel, harsh and sinister, yet with such depth of feeling, and so schematically beautiful as he stands framed in a panel at the back of the stage gravely contemplating the apparent happiness of his employers?[59]

Crab on this occasion was played by Blackie, a good-natured mongrel, who, as Peter Roberts comments, was "a cur of the kind that would win a sneer at Crufts and a very big bone everywhere else":[60]

He [Stewart] recites most of his lines in the company of a big dog, Blackie, and he needs all his talent and experience to prevent Blackie from stealing several scenes. In one of Launce's long speeches Blackie emitted a big yawn. It nearly brought the house down.[61]

Critics frequently comment on the resemblance between man and dog. In John Barton's double bill, it was the dog's resemblance to the director which struck a number of reviewers, as well as its appearance in *Titus*:

When John Barton assigned the role of Crab against considerable canine opposition to an old English sheepdog named Heidi, there were murmurings in Stratford about "mirror images." Barton himself now affects a shaggy, rumpled appearance from his grizzled head to his Hush Puppies.*[62]

Richard Moore as Lance in Thacker's immensely popular production achieved a remarkable comic performance: "a blend of Leonard Rossiter, Tony Hancock and a big-eared Victorian toby jug, never more hilarious than when he is lugubriously berating a dog which,

---

*"Hush Puppies" is the brand name for a type of casual brown suede shoe with a basset hound as its logo.

on opening night, stood and implored the audience for rescue, death, anything but this."[63]

Margaret Ingram's evocative account concluded,

> But I have not mentioned Launce (Richard Moore) and his dog Crab (Woolly) who perhaps contributed most of all, Launce with his lugubrious humour and Crab who evinced a look between dullness and despair at being confined on a brightly lit stage when he might have been enjoying a dog's life elsewhere but who nevertheless seemed to appreciate that, this being a British audience, he received the greatest applause of the evening.[64]

Mark Hadfield's performance in Edward Hall's production was also singled out: "The most entertaining scenes of *Two Gentlemen* belong to Launce (Mark Hadfield is a fine clown) and his faithful, similarly downbeat mongrel, Crab."[65] Robert Smallwood described him as a "sad and knowing Launce," and Cassie's Crab as "a most economically paced performance."[66] In Buffini's 2004 production Lance was played by Andrew Melville, "a lachrymose Scot and his dog Crab, an elderly Irish wolfhound, whose only crime on stage was to yawn—*not* fair comment."[67]

Conclusion

In his discussion of the play, quoted in the 1992 program, Stanley Wells concludes that it is "a failure" but it is "far from being a total failure."

> [The] most important reason for the play's success is that how-ever immature he may be in other ways, he [Shakespeare] is already completely assured as a writer of comic prose, of lyri-cal verse, and even sometimes of genuine dramatic verse. When we try to get below the surface of the play, we find that it rests on shaky foundations. In these circumstances, the best thing to do seems to be to come up to the surface again and examine that.[68]

Successful productions have done just that; they have attended to the play's surface, updating it with contemporary settings and ideas to suggest modern parallels, which, far from detracting from the text have enabled its virtues of vigor, freshness, and lyrical charm to shine through.

THE DIRECTOR'S CUT: INTERVIEWS WITH DAVID THACKER AND EDWARD HALL

David Thacker was born in Northamptonshire in 1950. He was the artistic director of the Young Vic from 1984 to 1993, where his directorial achievements included *The Jail Diary of Albie Sachs, Stags and Hens, Macbeth, Hamlet, Measure for Measure, The Enemies Within, The Crucible, Romeo and Juliet, A Midsummer Night's Dream, Some Kind of Hero, Ghosts, Julius Caesar,* and *Who's Afraid of Virginia Woolf?* He directed the production of *The Two Gentlemen of Verona* discussed below for the RSC in 1991, and became director-in-residence for the company in 1993. He is a prolific television director and is currently the artistic director of the Octagon Theatre, Bolton. He has won Olivier Awards for Best Director (*Pericles*) and Best Revival (*Pericles*) and the London Fringe Award for Best Director (*Ghosts*) and Best Production (*Who's Afraid of Virginia Woolf?*).

    Edward Hall, son of the RSC's founder Sir Peter Hall, was born in 1967 and trained at Leeds University and the Mountview Theatre School before cutting his teeth at the Watermill Theatre in the 1990s. His first Shakespearean success was a production of *Othello* in 1995, though he used the experience as inspiration to found Propeller, an all-male theater company with whom he directed *The Comedy of Errors* and *Henry V*, which ran together in repertory during the 1997–98 season, and *Twelfth Night* in 1999, all at the Watermill. In 1998 he made his directorial debut with the RSC on the production of *The Two Gentlemen of Verona* discussed below, and went on to work with the company on *Henry V* in 2000–01 and *Julius Caesar* the following season. In between *Henry* and *Caesar,* Hall returned to the Watermill to direct *Rose Rage,* his (in)famous and celebrated abattoir-set adaptation of the *Henry VI* trilogy. He has continued to work with

Propeller on such productions as *A Midsummer Night's Dream* in 2003 and *Twelfth Night* and *The Taming of the Shrew* in 2007, becoming artistic director of the Hampstead Theatre in 2010.

Two Gents is regarded as an early play, an apprentice piece, in which characters and plot are not fully realized; did this perception affect your production in any way?

Thacker: I think it's an exceptionally good play. I've liked it since the first time I encountered it. There may have been people who thought, because of the imaginative choices we took in our production, that I felt the play needed shoring up in some way, but that was never the case. I think it is self-evidently a young person's play, written by a young man; it has a lot of the enthusiasm and spontaneity of youth, and also the innocence of youth. I felt that the style of it was very pure and shows Shakespeare at an advanced stage in his development.

Hall: No, not really. There is a youthful exuberance and energy about the writing that I imagine is the expression of a young writer first discovering the possibilities of drama. Like *The Taming of the Shrew*, another early play, and to a degree *The Comedy of Errors*, there is a wonderfully warm, enthusiastic style that is all about youth, about young people. When you embrace that it's exciting to feel the real spirit of youth, as embodied by the four principles, coming off the page. When you feel that, suddenly all those academic worries and concerns about the printed text recede in the "doing" of it. We certainly found that when we were working on it.

Many of the most successful productions have updated the play and set it in recognizable modern locations; when and where was your production set?

Thacker: As a director I need to imagine a world in which I believe the events of the play could plausibly take place. It's sometimes difficult to explain why it is that a particular way of staging or presenting a play comes into your mind. In this particular case I can remember vividly that I was lying in bed reading the play, thinking about the possibility of doing it, and the songs of the late twenties and early thirties came into my mind. Years before I had done a play about life in Lancashire between the two world wars—it was called *The Rose Between Two Thorns*—which consisted entirely of transcribed verbatim material. In it we had used a lot of songs from the period, so those songs were quite familiar to me and I had become very fond of many of them. I found myself hearing those songs as I was reading *Two Gents* and it struck me that some of the lyrics and also the melodies of the songs seemed to be a very close correlative to what Shakespeare was investigating in this play. The innocence of some of these Cole Porter and Gershwin songs, and some of those other songs from the period, suddenly made me wonder whether this play would work well if set in that period.

At that time I was not particularly clear in my own mind that one might use songs from the period. I was still having this little imaginative adventure while reading the play, but then I read it through again more carefully and began to feel that the period would work extremely well for the play.

I started to check out the dates of composition of the songs and talk to the designer, Shelagh Keegan, about whether or not she felt the play would work well aesthetically in that era. We looked at what kind of clothes people were wearing at the time. The next piece of the jigsaw arrived when I received a letter from Guy Woolfenden, who had composed music for every play by Shakespeare at the RSC apart from *Two Gents*. He wrote me a very charming letter to ask whether I would be prepared to consider him to compose the music for the production. I phoned him up and said, "Well, of course I'd be privileged if you were to do it, Guy, but I should tell you that I've got this very strong idea about how I'd like to do the play and you may think it's terrible; and if you did I wouldn't be offended but you might feel that it wasn't an idea that you would like to run with as composer." I explained the idea and almost immediately he said, "My father had a band in that period and I love that music, and I think it's the most fantastic idea." We met up, and he brought along with him well over one hundred examples of songs from the period, and we convinced ourselves very rapidly that this was going to be a way of enabling the play to have a full and vivid expression.

Some people may not agree, but I can say with total conviction and honesty that the wish to set it in that context, using that music, was because we respected the play enormously—not because we thought it needed improving in some way. The music became like an additional design feature. We had a band on stage the whole time and a female crooner singing, and sometimes the songs would actually underscore the text. It was an organic process whereby we decided to run with that as a settled concept. I have to say that of all the productions that I have ever directed, it is one that I have been most proud of, because I think it reached the audience in a really powerful way. After playing at the Swan and then the Barbican it had a national tour and also became the first play by Shakespeare for many years to transfer to the West End.

Hall: Our production was set in modern-day Italy. It was a very stylish, fashionable setting; that was the touchstone to the production. The wood was a wasteland where we stripped everything away, almost like the side of an autoroute somewhere in the middle of Italy. We kept a contemporary Italian feel to it which fed the play in a very satisfactory way.

The play has an intrinsic interest in twoness: two gents, two girls, two fathers, two comic servants, and so on; how did you explore/exploit this patterning?

Thacker: Not in any conscious way. So much of Shakespeare is to do with antithesis, both in his linguistic techniques and within the language that he chooses to use. He clearly sets up opposites but it wasn't something that we particularly highlighted, we just allowed it to play out as it was expressed.

Of course, the two servants are wonderfully contrasting and they play brilliantly. Richard Moore gave, I think, one of his favorite performances playing Lance and we were blessed with the most wonderful dog, Woolley, who sadly has passed away now. Woolley and Richard were so popular and made such a strong impression that there was even a cartoon in *The Times* of the two of them.

Hall: We didn't make a particular effort to exploit it, but yes, it has a pair of everything, apart from a pair of dogs—so you could argue

7. David Thacker's 1991 RSC production with Richard Moore as Lance with Woolley the dog as Crab: "Richard Moore gave I think one of his favorite performances playing Lance and we were blessed with a wonderful dog, Woolley . . . Woolley and Richard were so popular and made such a strong impression that there was even a cartoon in *The Times* of the two of them."

that the whole thing is set up to make Crab work as best as possible!' The early plays have a lot of pairs in them; possibly the death of his twin son, Hamnet, is fresh in his mind [the other twin, a daughter, Judith, survived]. It's also to do with two halves of the self. Twins represent two people feeling different things and disagreeing and then coming together to agree. You are split down the middle, and when people come together and understand each other they become more whole as people, as individuals.

Same-sex friendships seem stronger and more satisfying than heterosexual love in this play; did you see homoeroticism and male bonding as in conflict with romance, and how did you play it?

Thacker: Our belief when we were working on the play was that these young men had hugely strong feelings for each other, but I don't think any of us felt that those would have been consummated sexually or, indeed, repressed homoerotically. We all believed when we were working on the play that it was fundamentally to do with heterosexual love but with men who were very close and loved each other very powerfully. The conflict that arises between them is more powerful because of the strength of their love. But I don't think we ever saw it as homoerotic.

Hall: No. You have to understand that Elizabethans didn't categorize sexuality in the way that we do. We always make the terrible mistake of imposing our notions of sexuality onto sixteenth-century England. The idea of love was very highly evolved in Elizabethan society, whether it was physical love or spiritual love. A relationship between two men could be seen to embody the highest form of spiritual love. It doesn't have to engender something physical and it certainly doesn't necessarily have to make a comment on the particular sexuality of the person. Shakespeare writes about love in all its forms, but doesn't reduce it to being about sexuality. Running all the way through his plays he challenges conservative notions of sexuality: show me somebody who loves a woman and I will show that same man loving a man. I think I have always approached his work like that. I directed *Two Gentlemen of Verona* back in 1998 and I remember feeling that you're dealing with different kinds of love. It's to do with being true to somebody as much as it is to do with something physical. It becomes something physical in the last scene, and I remember us looking closely at the book of courtly love, looking at pictures by Hilliard, trying to get under the skin of the whole culture of courtly love at the time, so that we didn't reduce it to contemporary terms and miss what was really going on.

For modern audiences (and perhaps for early modern ones too), there's a difficult moment in Act 5 when Valentine calmly offers his beloved Silvia to his friend, her would-be rapist, Proteus; how did your production understand and deal with this moment?

Thacker: For a lot of people the play hinges on the attempted rape and the nature of redemption and forgiveness. I was incredibly fortunate to have a really exceptional young company of actors. The central quartet of the actors were Finbar Lynch and Hugh Bon-neville, both of whom have become major actors now, and Saskia Reeves and Clare Holman, both of whom were young, very talented actors and ever since have had distinguished careers. So I had four brilliant young actors at the heart of it and they all bought into it being a play about redemption and forgiveness. So many of Shake-speare's plays—and certainly his mature and brilliant plays in later life, culminating in *The Winter's Tale*—are about redemption and for-giveness and being prepared to actually accept an apology when it is truly meant. I think we all believed that Valentine's forgiveness of Proteus was absolutely credible and, for me, the actors demonstrated that to be true, irrespective of how it might read on the page.

I still believe very powerfully that is what Shakespeare was intend-ing to achieve. Although he would have done it much more effec-tively later in his life, nevertheless it is very moving and very powerful, not least because of its innocence. It is a play written by a young person about young people and it is very powerful because of that.

Hall: When you go out into the wasteland you discover the truth; you leave the confines of court society and strip away all artifice, and you come down to the truth of your feelings and how you really are. When we rehearsed it we made sure that we didn't play it faster than the actors could feel it, and it explained itself in performance. If you play it very quickly and just drive through it, it all seems glib and sud-denly the play means nothing. Clearly that is not Shakespeare's intention, so you have to invest as deeply as you can in what happens in the wasteland to both of them and not play it too quickly—not just the lines, but the space between the lines—so when we arrived at that moment it felt very natural for what it was. The question is rather like asking how do you do *The Taming of the Shrew?* How does Kate capitulate in the last scene? If you haven't got the rest of the play right, you can't do that scene. That is particularly true of Shake-speare. Act 5 of Shakespeare is like a set of dominoes going down: if they haven't hit each other just right in the preceding four acts, you find yourself having completely misarticulated what he was intend-ing. If you set off on the wrong track then the further you travel, the further away you find yourself from where you need to be. So when you get to Act 5 in *Two Gents* you are suddenly in the woods and that moment seems ridiculous, or you get to Act 5 of *The Taming of the Shrew* and Kate's capitulation seems ridiculous. But I do believe that if you have got the play right, then those moments explain themselves and I like to think ours did.

Music has often featured prominently in productions, perhaps to cover for the play's perceived weaknesses; were you tempted by this strategy?

Thacker: See answer to question two.

Hall: We did use music, some recorded and some live, but it wasn't a musical. When Proteus serenaded Silvia he hired the best tenor he could find, so it wasn't actually him singing. I imagine he got someone from the local opera company and paid them a lot of money, which gave us an excuse to get a rather wonderful singer to play that moment for him.

The Outlaws always seem very genteel (our edition has a stage direction "Outlaws confer privately" which seems to sum them up), and Valentine an especially unlikely captain of an outlaw band; how realistically did you treat your Outlaws?

Thacker: We treated them reasonably realistically. The challenge was more making them credible within this musical genre that we'd segued into at that moment in the show. When Silvia was running away the rising of both lyrics and melody in "Do You Love Me As I Love You" is the thing that remains powerfully in my memory for that moment. So I think we downplayed the Outlaws a bit.

Shakespeare reputedly disliked dogs and W. C. Fields famously recommended never working with children or animals; how did you find directing a dog?

Thacker: We had a charity gala event for hearing dogs for the deaf that was attended by Princess Anne. I sat next to Princess Anne during the performance and she didn't really say much until we got to the point in the action when Lance used to press Crab's bottom down to make him sit. Immediately he would always stand up and it would get a laugh every night. At that point, she turned to me and said "Lurchers won't sit!" That was her main comment on the show until the end, when she was very sweet and polite: He was a lovely dog and he got on so well with Richard. In fact the owners of the dog became very good friends of Richard. Richard handled Woolley brilliantly and so, far from it being a problem, it was a massive bonus for the production. I think all of us look back on the production with an enormous fondness for Woolley and admiration for the way the two of them worked together.

Hall: The dog was wonderful. On the first preview he walked on and looked out at the audience and then turned his back and lay down, which brought the house down. Mark Hadfield, who was playing Lance, had a high old time after that. Once Ben Ormerod, the lighting designer, and I had got the lighting just right so that the dog

8. Edward Hall's 1998 RSC production in the Swan with Mark Hadfield as Lance and Cassie as Crab: "this big wonderful mangy Irish wolfhound crossbreed, which I think he has to be, and he was brilliant. The wonderful thing about Crab is that it's not just about the dog: it's about the dog and Lance. If Lance is on the money, which Mark Hadfield was, then if the dog does something you can use it, and if the dog does nothing you can use it."

wasn't being dazzled he would sit and look at the audience. He was this big wonderful mangy Irish wolfhound crossbreed, which I think he has to be, and he was brilliant. The wonderful thing about Crab is that it's not just about the dog: it's about the dog and Lance. If Lance is on the money, which Mark Hadfield was, then if the dog does something you can use it, and if the dog does nothing you can use it. But you have to not fight what the dog does. When Crab's understudy went on a couple of times we did have a few problems because he was a slightly small yappy thing, and every time Dominic Rowan, who was playing Proteus, went close to him he yapped wildly. After a couple of shows Dominic realized this and used it to great comic effect.

SHAKESPEARE'S CAREER IN THE THEATER

BEGINNINGS

William Shakespeare was an extraordinarily intelligent man who was born and died in an ordinary market town in the English Midlands. He lived an uneventful life in an eventful age. Born in April 1564, he was the eldest son of John Shakespeare, a glove maker who was prominent on the town council until he fell into financial difficulties. Young William was educated at the local grammar in Stratford-upon-Avon, Warwickshire, where he gained a thorough grounding in the Latin language, the art of rhetoric and classical poetry. He married Ann Hathaway and had three children (Susanna, then the twins Hamnet and Judith) before his twenty-first birthday: an exceptionally young age for the period. We do not know how he supported his family in the mid-1580s.

Like many clever country boys, he moved to the city in order to make his way in the world. Like many creative people, he found a career in the entertainment business. Public playhouses and professional full-time acting companies reliant on the market for their income were born in Shakespeare's childhood. When he arrived in London as a man, sometime in the late 1580s, a new phenomenon was in the making: the actor who is so successful that he becomes a "star." The word did not exist in its modern sense, but the pattern is recognizable: audiences went to the theater not so much to see a particular show as to witness the comedian Richard Tarlton or the dramatic actor Edward Alleyn.

Shakespeare was an actor before he was a writer. It appears not to have been long before he realized that he was never going to grow into a great comedian like Tarlton or a great tragedian like Alleyn. Instead, he found a role within his company as the man who patched up old plays, breathing new life, new dramatic twists, into tired repertory pieces. He paid close attention to the work of the university-educated dramatists who were writing history plays and tragedies for the public stage in a style more ambitious, sweeping, and poetically grand than anything that had been seen before. But he may also have noted that what his friend and rival Ben Jonson would call "Marlowe's mighty line" sometimes faltered in the mode of comedy. Going to university, as Christopher Marlowe did, was all well and good for honing the arts of rhetorical elaboration and classical allusion, but it could lead to a loss of the common touch. To stay close to a large segment of the potential audience for public theater, it was necessary to write for clowns as well as kings and to intersperse the flights of poetry with the humor of the tavern, the privy, and the brothel: Shakespeare was the first to establish himself early in his career as an equal master of tragedy, comedy, and history. He realized that theater could be the medium to make the national past available to a wider audience than the elite who could afford to read large history books: his signature early works include not only the classical tragedy *Titus Andronicus* but also the sequence of English historical plays on the Wars of the Roses.

He also invented a new role for himself, that of in-house company dramatist. Where his peers and predecessors had to sell their plays to the theater managers on a poorly paid piecework basis, Shakespeare took a percentage of the box-office income. The Lord Chamberlain's Men constituted themselves in 1594 as a joint stock company, with the profits being distributed among the core actors who had invested as sharers. Shakespeare acted himself—he appears in the cast lists of some of Ben Jonson's plays as well as the list of actors' names at the beginning of his own collected works—but his principal duty was to write two or three plays a year for the company. By holding shares, he was effectively earning himself a royalty on his work, something no author had ever done before in England. When the Lord Chamberlain's Men collected their fee for performance at court in the Christmas season of 1594, three of them went along to the Treasurer of the Chamber: not just Richard Burbage the tragedian and Will Kempe the clown, but also Shakespeare the scriptwriter. That was something new.

The next four years were the golden period in Shakespeare's

career, though overshadowed by the death of his only son, Hamnet, age eleven, in 1596. In his early thirties and in full command of both his poetic and his theatrical medium, he perfected his art of comedy, while also developing his tragic and historical writing in new ways. In 1598, Francis Meres, a Cambridge University graduate with his finger on the pulse of the London literary world, praised Shakespeare for his excellence across the genres:

> As Plautus and Seneca are accounted the best for comedy and tragedy among the Latins, so Shakespeare among the English is the most excellent in both kinds for the stage; for comedy, witness his *Gentlemen of Verona*, his *Errors*, his *Love Labours Lost*, his *Love Labours Won*, his *Midsummer Night Dream* and his *Merchant of Venice*: for tragedy his *Richard the 2*, *Richard the 3*, *Henry the 4*, *King John*, *Titus Andronicus* and his *Romeo and Juliet*.

For Meres, as for the many writers who praised the "honey-flowing vein" of *Venus and Adonis* and *Lucrece*, narrative poems written when the theaters were closed due to plague in 1593–94, Shakespeare was marked above all by his linguistic skill, by the gift of turning elegant poetic phrases.

PLAYHOUSES

Elizabethan playhouses were "thrust" or "one-room" theaters. To understand Shakespeare's original theatrical life, we have to forget about the indoor theater of later times, with its proscenium arch and curtain that would be opened at the beginning and closed at the end of each act. In the proscenium arch theater, stage and auditorium are effectively two separate rooms: the audience looks from one world into another as if through the imaginary "fourth wall" framed by the proscenium. The picture-frame stage, together with the elaborate scenic effects and backdrops beyond it, created the illusion of a self-contained world—especially once nineteenth-century developments in the control of artificial lighting meant that the auditorium could be darkened and the spectators made to focus on the lighted stage. Shakespeare, by contrast, wrote for a bare platform stage with a standing audience gathered around it in a courtyard in full daylight. The audience were always conscious of themselves and their fellow spectators, and they shared the same "room" as the actors. A sense of immediate presence and the creation of rapport with the audience were all-important. The actor could not afford to imagine he was in a closed world, with silent witnesses dutifully observing him from the darkness.

Shakespeare's theatrical career began at the Rose Theatre in Southwark. The stage was wide and shallow, trapezoid in shape, like a lozenge. This design had a great deal of potential for the theatrical equivalent of cinematic split-screen effects, whereby one group of characters would enter at the door at one end of the tiring-house wall at the back of the stage and another group through the door at the other end, thus creating two rival tableaux. Many of the battle-heavy and faction-filled plays that premiered at the Rose have scenes of just this sort.

At the rear of the Rose stage, there were three capacious exits, each over ten feet wide. Unfortunately, the very limited excavation of a fragmentary portion of the original Globe site, in 1989, revealed nothing about the stage. The first Globe was built in 1599 with similar proportions to those of another theater, the Fortune, albeit that the former was polygonal and looked circular, whereas the latter was rectangular. The building contract for the Fortune survives and allows us to infer that the stage of the Globe was probably substantially wider than it was deep (perhaps forty-three feet wide and twenty-seven feet deep). It may well have been tapered at the front, like that of the Rose.

The capacity of the Globe was said to have been enormous, perhaps in excess of three thousand. It has been conjectured that about eight hundred people may have stood in the yard, with two thousand or more in the three layers of covered galleries. The other "public" playhouses were also of large capacity, whereas the indoor Blackfriars theater that Shakespeare's company began using in 1608—the former refectory of a monastery—had overall internal dimensions of a mere forty-six by sixty feet. It would have made for a much more intimate theatrical experience and had a much smaller capacity, probably of about six hundred people. Since they paid at least six-pence a head, the Blackfriars attracted a more select or "private" audience. The atmosphere would have been closer to that of an indoor performance before the court in the Whitehall Palace or at Richmond. That Shakespeare always wrote for indoor production at court as well as outdoor performance in the public theater should make us cautious about inferring, as some scholars have, that the opportunity provided by the intimacy of the Blackfriars led to a sig-nificant change toward a "chamber" style in his last plays—which, besides, were performed at both the Globe and the Blackfriars. After the occupation of the Blackfriars a five-act structure seems to have become more important to Shakespeare. That was because of artifi-cial lighting: there were musical interludes between the acts, while the candles were trimmed and replaced. Again, though, something similar must have been necessary for indoor court performances throughout his career.

Front of house there were the "gatherers" who collected the money from audience members: a penny to stand in the open-air yard, another penny for a place in the covered galleries, sixpence for the prominent "lord's rooms" to the side of the stage. In the indoor "pri-vate" theaters, gallants from the audience who fancied making themselves part of the spectacle sat on stools on the edge of the stage itself. Scholars debate as to how widespread this practice was in the public theaters such as the Globe. Once the audience were in place and the money counted, the gatherers were available to be extras on stage. That is one reason why battles and crowd scenes often come later rather than early in Shakespeare's plays. There was no formal prohibition upon performance by women, and there certainly were women among the gatherers, so it is not beyond the bounds of possi-bility that female crowd members were played by females.

The play began at two o'clock in the afternoon and the theater had to be cleared by five. After the main show, there would be a jig—which consisted not only of dancing, but also of knockabout comedy (it is the origin of the farcical "afterpiece" in the eighteenth-century theater). So the time available for a Shakespeare play was about two and a half hours, somewhere between the "two hours' traffic" men-tioned in the prologue to *Romeo and Juliet* and the "three hours' spectacle" referred to in the preface to the 1647 Folio of Beaumont and Fletcher's plays. The prologue to a play by Thomas Middleton refers to a thousand lines as "one hour's words," so the likelihood is that about two and a half thousand, or a maximum of three thousand lines made up the performed text. This is indeed the length of most of Shakespeare's comedies, whereas many of his tragedies and histories are much longer, raising the possibility that he wrote full scripts, possibly with eventual publication in mind, in the full knowledge that the stage version would be heavily cut. The short Quarto texts published in his lifetime—they used to be called "Bad" Quartos—provide fascinating evidence as to the kind of cutting that probably took place. So, for instance, the First Quarto of *Hamlet* neatly merges two occasions when Hamlet is overheard, the "Fishmonger" and the "nunnery" scenes.

The social composition of the audience was mixed. The poet Sir John Davies wrote of "A thousand townsmen, gentlemen and whores, / Porters and servingmen" who would "together throng" at the public playhouses. Though moralists associated female playgoing with adultery and the sex trade, many perfectly respectable citizens' wives were regular attendees. Some, no doubt, resembled the modern groupie: a story attested in two different sources has one citizen's wife making a postshow assignation with Richard Burbage and ending up in bed with Shakespeare—supposedly eliciting from the latter the quip that William the Conqueror was before Richard III. Defenders of theater liked to say that by witnessing the comeuppance of villains on the stage, audience members would repent of their own wrongdoings, but the reality is that most people went to the theater then, as they do now, for entertainment more than moral edification. Besides, it would be foolish to suppose that audiences behaved in a homogeneous way: a pamphlet of the 1630s tells of how two men went to see *Pericles* and one of them laughed while the other wept. Bishop John Hall complained that people went to church for the same reasons that they went to the theater: "for company, for custom, for recreation . . . to feed his eyes or his ears . . . or perhaps for sleep."

Men-about-town and clever young lawyers went to be seen as much as to see. In the modern popular imagination, shaped not least by *Shakespeare in Love* and the opening sequence of Laurence Olivier's *Henry V* film, the penny-paying groundlings stand in the yard hurling abuse or encouragement and hazelnuts or orange peel at the actors, while the sophisticates in the covered galleries appreciate Shakespeare's soaring poetry. The reality was probably the other way round. A "groundling" was a kind of fish, so the nickname suggests the penny audience standing below the level of the stage and gazing in silent open-mouthed wonder at the spectacle unfolding above them. The more difficult audience members, who kept up a running commentary of clever remarks on the performance and who occasionally got into quarrels with players, were the gallants. Like Hollywood movies in modern times, Elizabethan and Jacobean plays exercised a powerful influence on the fashion and behavior of the young. John Marston mocks the lawyers who would open their lips, perhaps to court a girl, and out would "flow / Naught but pure Juliet and Romeo."

THE ENSEMBLE AT WORK

In the absence of typewriters and photocopying machines, reading aloud would have been the means by which the company got to know a new play. The tradition of the playwright reading his complete script to the assembled company endured for generations. A copy would then have been taken to the Master of the Revels for licensing. The theater book-holder or prompter would then have copied the parts for distribution to the actors. A partbook consisted of the character's lines, with each speech preceded by the last three or four words of the speech before, the so-called "cue." These would have been taken away and studied or "conned." During this period of learning the parts, an actor might have had some one-to-one instruction, perhaps from the dramatist, perhaps from a senior actor who had played the same part before, and, in the case of an apprentice, from his master. A high percentage of Desdemona's lines occur in dialogue with Othello, of Lady Macbeth's with Macbeth, Cleopatra's with Antony, and Volumnia's with Coriolanus. The roles would almost certainly have been taken by the apprentice of the lead actor, usually Burbage, who delivers the majority of the cues. Given that

9. Hypothetical reconstruction of the interior of an Elizabethan playhouse during a performance.

apprentices lodged with their masters, there would have been ample opportunity for personal instruction, which may be what made it possible for young men to play such demanding parts.

After the parts were learned, there may have been no more than a single rehearsal before the first performance. With six different plays to be put on every week, there was no time for more. Actors, then, would go into a show with a very limited sense of the whole. The notion of a collective rehearsal process that is itself a process of discovery for the actors is wholly modern and would have been incomprehensible to Shakespeare and his original ensemble. Given the number of parts an actor had to hold in his memory, the forgetting of lines was probably more frequent than in the modern theater. The book-holder was on hand to prompt.

Backstage personnel included the property man, the tire-man who oversaw the costumes, call boys, attendants, and the musicians, who might play at various times from the main stage, the rooms above, and within the tiring-house. Scriptwriters sometimes made a nuisance of themselves backstage. There was often tension between the acting companies and the freelance playwrights from whom they purchased scripts: it was a smart move on the part of Shakespeare and the Lord Chamberlain's Men to bring the writing process in-house.

Scenery was limited, though sometimes set pieces were brought on (a bank of flowers, a bed, the mouth of hell). The trapdoor from below, the gallery stage above, and the curtained discovery space at the back allowed for an array of special effects: the rising of ghosts and apparitions, the descent of gods, dialogue between a character at a window and another at ground level, the revelation of a statue, or a pair of lovers playing at chess. Ingenious use could be made of props, as with the ass's head in *A Midsummer Night's Dream*. In a theater that does not clutter the stage with the material paraphernalia of everyday life, those objects that are deployed may take on powerful symbolic weight, as when Shylock bears his weighing scales in one hand and knife in the other, thus becoming a parody of the figure of Justice who traditionally bears a sword and a balance. Among the more significant items in the property cupboard of Shakespeare's company, there would have been a throne (the "chair of state"), joint stools, books, bottles, coins, purses, letters (which are brought on stage, read, or referred to on about eighty occasions in the complete works), maps, gloves, a set of stocks (in which Kent is put in *King Lear*), rings, rapiers, daggers, broadswords, staves, pistols, masks and vizards, heads and skulls, torches and tapers and lanterns, which served to signal night scenes on the daylit stage, a buck's head, an ass's head, animal costumes. Live animals also put in appearances, most notably the dog Crab in *The Two Gentlemen of Verona* and possibly a young polar bear in *The Winter's Tale*.

The costumes were the most important visual dimension of the play. Playwrights were paid between £2 and £6 per script, whereas Alleyn was not averse to paying £20 for "a black velvet cloak with sleeves embroidered all with silver and gold." No matter the period of the play, actors always wore contemporary costume. The excitement for the audience came not from any impression of historical accuracy, but from the richness of the attire and perhaps the transgressive thrill of the knowledge that here were commoners like themselves strutting in the costumes of courtiers in effective defiance of the strict sumptuary laws whereby in real life people had to wear the clothes that befitted their social station.

To an even greater degree than props, costumes could carry symbolic importance. Racial characteristics could be suggested: a breastplate and helmet for a Roman soldier, a turban for a Turk, long robes for exotic characters such as Moors, a gabardine for a Jew. The figure of Time, as in *The Winter's Tale*, would be equipped with hourglass, scythe and wings; Rumor, who speaks the prologue of *2 Henry IV*, wore a costume adorned with a thousand tongues. The wardrobe in the tiring house of the Globe would have contained much of the same stock as that of rival manager Philip Henslowe at the Rose: green gowns for outlaws and foresters, black for melancholy men such as Jaques and people in mourning such as the Countess in *All's Well That Ends Well* (at the beginning of *Hamlet*, the prince is still in mourning black when everyone else is in festive garb for the wedding of the new king), a gown and hood for a friar (or a feigned friar like the duke in *Measure for Measure*), blue coats and tawny to distinguish the followers of rival factions, a leather apron and ruler for a carpenter (as in the opening scene of *Julius Caesar*—and in *A Midsummer Night's Dream*, where this is the only sign that Peter Quince is a carpenter), a cockle hat with staff and a pair of sandals for a pilgrim or palmer (the disguise assumed by Helen in *All's Well*), bodices and kirtles with farthingales beneath for the boys who are to be dressed as girls. A gender switch such as that of Rosalind or Jessica seems to have taken between fifty and eighty lines of dialogue—Viola does not resume her "maiden weeds," but remains in her boy's costume to the end of *Twelfth Night* because a change would have slowed down the action at just the moment it was speeding to a climax. Henslowe's inventory also included "a robe for to go invisible": Oberon, Puck, and Ariel must have had something similar.

As the costumes appealed to the eyes, so there was music for the ears. Comedies included many songs. Desdemona's willow song, perhaps a late addition to the text, is a rare and thus exceptionally poignant example from tragedy. Trumpets and tuckets sounded for ceremonial entrances, drums denoted an army on the march. Background music could create atmosphere, as at the beginning of *Twelfth Night*, during the lovers' dialogue near the end of *The Mer-*

chant of Venice, when the statue seemingly comes to life in *The Winter's Tale*, and for the revival of Pericles and of Lear (in the Quarto text, but not the Folio). The haunting sound of the hautboy suggested a realm beyond the human, as when the god Hercules is imagined deserting Mark Antony. Dances symbolized the harmony of the end of a comedy—though in Shakespeare's world of mingled joy and sorrow, someone is usually left out of the circle.

The most important resource was, of course, the actors themselves. They needed many skills: in the words of one contemporary commentator, "dancing, activity, music, song, elocution, ability of body, memory, skill of weapon, pregnancy of wit." Their bodies were as significant as their voices. Hamlet tells the player to "suit the action to the word, the word to the action": moments of strong emotion, known as "passions," relied on a repertoire of dramatic gestures as well as a modulation of the voice. When Titus Andronicus has had his hand chopped off, he asks "How can I grace my talk, / Wanting a hand to give it action?" A pen portrait of "The Character of an Excellent Actor" by the dramatist John Webster is almost certainly based on his impression of Shakespeare's leading man, Richard Burbage: "By a full and significant action of body, he charms our attention: sit in a full theatre, and you will think you see so many lines drawn from the circumference of so many ears, whiles the actor is the centre . . . ."

Though Burbage was admired above all others, praise was also heaped upon the apprentice players whose alto voices fitted them for the parts of women. A spectator at Oxford in 1610 records how the audience were reduced to tears by the pathos of Desdemona's death. The puritans who fumed about the biblical prohibition upon cross-dressing and the encouragement to sodomy constituted by the sight of an adult male kissing a teenage boy on stage were a small minority. Little is known, however, about the characteristics of the leading apprentices in Shakespeare's company. It may perhaps be inferred that one was a lot taller than the other, since Shakespeare often wrote for a pair of female friends, one tall and fair, the other short and dark (Helena and Hermia, Rosalind and Celia, Beatrice and Hero).

We know little about Shakespeare's own acting roles—an early allusion indicates that he often took royal parts, and a venerable tradition gives him old Adam in *As You Like It* and the ghost of old King Hamlet. Save for Burbage's lead roles and the generic part of the clown, all such castings are mere speculation. We do not even know for sure whether the original Falstaff was Will Kempe or another actor who specialized in comic roles, Thomas Pope.

Kempe left the company in early 1599. Tradition has it that he fell out with Shakespeare over the matter of excessive improvisation. He was replaced by Robert Armin, who was less of a clown and more of a cerebral wit: this explains the difference between such parts as Lancelet Gobbo and Dogberry, which were written for Kempe, and the more verbally sophisticated Feste and Lear's Fool, which were written for Armin.

One thing that is clear from surviving "plots" or storyboards of plays from the period is that a degree of doubling was necessary. *2 Henry VI* has over sixty speaking parts, but more than half of the characters only appear in a single scene and most scenes have only six to eight speakers. At a stretch, the play could be performed by thirteen actors. When Thomas Platter saw *Julius Caesar* at the Globe in 1599, he noted that there were about fifteen. Why doesn't Paris go to the Capulet ball in *Romeo and Juliet*? Perhaps because he was doubled with Mercutio, who does. In *The Winter's Tale*, Mamillius might have come back as Perdita and Antigonus been doubled by Camillo, making the partnership with Paulina at the end a very neat touch. Titania and Oberon are often played by the same pair as Hippolyta and Theseus, suggesting a symbolic matching of the rulers of the worlds of night and day, but it is questionable whether there would have been time for the necessary costume changes. As so often, one is left in a realm of tantalizing speculation.

THE KING'S MAN

On Queen Elizabeth's death in 1603, the new king, James I, who had held the Scottish throne as James VI since he had been an infant, immediately took the Lord Chamberlain's Men under his direct patronage. Henceforth they would be the King's Men, and for the rest of Shakespeare's career they were favored with far more court performances than any of their rivals. There even seem to have been rumors early in the reign that Shakespeare and Burbage were being considered for knighthoods, an unprecedented honor for mere actors—and one that in the event was not accorded to a member of the profession for nearly three hundred years, when the title was bestowed upon Henry Irving, the leading Shakespearean actor of Queen Victoria's reign.

Shakespeare's productivity rate slowed in the Jacobean years, not because of age or some personal trauma, but because there were frequent outbreaks of plague, causing the theaters to be closed for long periods. The King's Men were forced to spend many months on the road. Between November 1603 and 1608, they were to be found at various towns in the south and Midlands, though Shakespeare probably did not tour with them by this time. He had bought a large house back home in Stratford and was accumulating other property. He may indeed have stopped acting soon after the new king took the throne. With the London theaters closed so much of the time and a large repertoire on the stocks, Shakespeare seems to have focused his energies on writing a few long and complex tragedies that could have been played on demand at court: *Othello*, *King Lear*, *Antony and Cleopatra*, *Coriolanus*, and *Cymbeline* are among his longest and poetically grandest plays. *Macbeth* only survives in a shorter text, which shows signs of adaptation after Shakespeare's death. The bitterly satirical *Timon of Athens*, apparently a collaboration with Thomas Middleton that may have failed on the stage, also belongs to this period. In comedy, too, he wrote longer and morally darker works than in the Elizabethan period, pushing at the very bounds of the form in *Measure for Measure* and *All's Well That Ends Well*.

From 1608 onward, when the King's Men began occupying the indoor Blackfriars playhouse (as a winter house, meaning that they only used the outdoor Globe in summer?), Shakespeare turned to a more romantic style. His company had a great success with a revived and altered version of an old pastoral play called *Mucedorus*. It even featured a bear. The younger dramatist John Fletcher, meanwhile, sometimes working in collaboration with Francis Beaumont, was pioneering a new style of tragicomedy, a mix of romance and royalism laced with intrigue and pastoral excursions. Shakespeare experimented with this idiom in *Cymbeline* and it was presumably with his blessing that Fletcher eventually took over as the King's Men's company dramatist. The two writers apparently collaborated on three plays in the years 1612–14: a lost romance called *Cardenio* (based on the love-madness of a character in Cervantes' *Don Quixote*), *Henry VIII* (originally staged with the title "All Is True"), and *The Two Noble Kinsmen*, a dramatization of Chaucer's "Knight's Tale." These were written after Shakespeare's two final solo-authored plays, *The Winter's Tale*, a self-consciously old-fashioned work dramatizing the pastoral romance of his old enemy Robert Greene, and *The Tempest*, which at one and the same time drew together multiple theatrical traditions, diverse reading and contemporary interest in the fate of a ship that had been wrecked on the way to the New World.

The collaborations with Fletcher suggest that Shakespeare's career ended with a slow fade rather than the sudden retirement supposed by the nineteenth-century Romantic critics who read Prospero's epilogue to *The Tempest* as Shakespeare's personal farewell to his art. In the last few years of his life Shakespeare certainly spent more of his time in Stratford-upon-Avon, where he became further involved in property dealing and litigation. But his London life also continued. In 1613 he made his first major London property purchase: a freehold house in the Blackfriars district, close to his company's indoor theater. *The Two Noble Kinsmen* may have been written as late as 1614, and Shakespeare was in London on business a little over a year before he died of an unknown cause at home in Stratford-upon-Avon in 1616, probably on his fifty-second birthday.

About half the sum of his works were published in his lifetime, in texts of variable quality. A few years after his death, his fellow actors began putting together an authorized edition of his complete *Comedies, Histories and Tragedies*. It appeared in 1623, in large "Folio" format. This collection of thirty-six plays gave Shakespeare his immortality. In the words of his fellow dramatist Ben Jonson, who contributed two poems of praise at the start of the Folio, the body of his work made him "a monument without a tomb":

And art alive still while thy book doth live
And we have wits to read and praise to give . . .
He was not of an age, but for all time!

SHAKESPEARE'S WORKS: A CHRONOLOGY

1589–91	*? Arden of Faversham* (possible part authorship)
1589–92	*The Taming of the Shrew*
1589–92	*? Edward the Third* (possible part authorship)
1591	*The Second Part of Henry the Sixth*, originally called *The First Part of the Contention betwixt the Two Famous Houses of York and Lancaster* (element of coauthorship possible)
1591	*The Third Part of Henry the Sixth*, originally called *The True Tragedy of Richard Duke of York* (element of co-authorship probable)
1591–92	*The Two Gentlemen of Verona*
1591–92; perhaps revised 1594	*The Lamentable Tragedy of Titus Andronicus* (probably cowritten with, or revising an earlier version by, George Peele)
1592	*The First Part of Henry the Sixth*, probably with Thomas Nashe and others
1592/94	*King Richard the Third*
1593	*Venus and Adonis* (poem)
1593–94	*The Rape of Lucrece* (poem)
1593–1608	*Sonnets* (154 poems, published 1609 with *A Lover's Complaint*, a poem of disputed authorship)
1592–94/ 1600–03	*Sir Thomas More* (a single scene for a play originally by Anthony Munday, with other revisions by Henry Chettle, Thomas Dekker, and Thomas Heywood)
1594	*The Comedy of Errors*
1595	*Love's Labour's Lost*

1595–97	*Love's Labour's Won* (a lost play, unless the original title for another comedy)
1595–96	*A Midsummer Night's Dream*
1595–96	*The Tragedy of Romeo and Juliet*
1595–96	*King Richard the Second*
1595–97	*The Life and Death of King John* (possibly earlier)
1596–97	*The Merchant of Venice*
1596–97	*The First Part of Henry the Fourth*
1597–98	*The Second Part of Henry the Fourth*
1598	*Much Ado About Nothing*
1598–99	*The Passionate Pilgrim* (20 poems, some not by Shakespeare)
1599	*The Life of Henry the Fifth*
1599	"To the Queen" (epilogue for a court performance)
1599	*As You Like It*
1599	*The Tragedy of Julius Caesar*
1600–01	*The Tragedy of Hamlet, Prince of Denmark* (perhaps revising an earlier version)
1600–01	*The Merry Wives of Windsor* (perhaps revising version of 1597–99)
1601	"Let the Bird of Loudest Lay" (poem, known since 1807 as "The Phoenix and Turtle" [turtledove])
1601	*Twelfth Night, or What You Will*
1601–02	*The Tragedy of Troilus and Cressida*
1604	*The Tragedy of Othello, the Moor of Venice*
1604	*Measure for Measure*
1605	*All's Well That Ends Well*
1605	*The Life of Timon of Athens*, with Thomas Middleton
1605–06	*The Tragedy of King Lear*
1605–08	? contribution to *The Four Plays in One* (lost, except for *A Yorkshire Tragedy*, mostly by Thomas Middleton)

1606	*The Tragedy of Macbeth* (surviving text has additional scenes by Thomas Middleton)
1606–07	*The Tragedy of Antony and Cleopatra*
1608	*The Tragedy of Coriolanus*
1608	*Pericles, Prince of Tyre*, with George Wilkins
1610	*The Tragedy of Cymbeline*
1611	*The Winter's Tale*
1611	*The Tempest*
1612–13	*Cardenio*, with John Fletcher (survives only in later adaptation called *Double Falsehood* by Lewis Theobald)
1613	*Henry VIII (All Is True)*, with John Fletcher
1613–14	*The Two Noble Kinsmen*, with John Fletcher

FURTHER READING AND VIEWING

CRITICAL APPROACHES

Berry, Ralph, *Shakespeare's Comedies: Explorations in Form* (1972). Chapter II, "Love and Friendship," offers a still valid, highly critical reading of the play and the character of Valentine, pp. 40–53.

Friedman, Michael D., *"The World Must Be Peopled": Shakespeare's Comedies of Forgiveness* (2002). Argues that this represents a subgenre of Shakespearean comedy; chapter 2 focuses on the character of Proteus in *Two Gents*, pp. 41–75.

Gay, Penny, *Cambridge Introduction to Shakespeare's Comedies* (2008). Useful overview of comedies; chapter 3, "Courtly Lovers and the Real World," discusses *Two Gents*, pp. 35–57.

Leggatt, Alexander, *Shakespeare's Comedy of Love* (1974). Dated but still relevant introduction to Shakespeare's romantic comedies; chapter 2 on *Two Gents*.

Mangan, Michael, *A Preface to Shakespeare's Comedies 1594–1603* (1996). Useful overview of context and practices of Elizabethan comedy with a short introduction to *Two Gents*, pp. 129–33.

Mason, Pamela, ed., *Shakespeare: Early Comedies* Casebook Series (1995). Part 3 on *Two Gents*: selection of early critical essays including Pope, Johnson, and Hazlitt, plus three more recent studies.

Ryan, Kiernan, *Shakespeare's Comedies* (2009). Chapter 3, "Dancing Leviathans: *The Two Gentlemen of Verona*," offers a lively, sympathetic introduction to the play, pp. 39–55.

Schlueter, June, ed., *Two Gentlemen of Verona: Critical Essays* (1996). Broad range of critical essays from Samuel Johnson and William Hazlitt up to 1996 in Part I; Part II has a shorter section with a selection of reviews of productions from 1821 to Thacker's 1991 RSC production.

THE PLAY IN PERFORMANCE

Carlisle, Carol J., and Patty S. Derrick, "*The Two Gentlemen of Verona* on Stage: Protean Problems and Protean Solutions," in *Shakespeare's Sweet Thunder*, ed. Michael J. Collins (1997). Useful stage history of the play.

Holland, Peter, *English Shakespeares* (1997). Perceptive detailed review of Thacker's RSC production set within the wider context of contemporary Shakespearean performance, pp. 87–91.

Schlueter, June, ed., *Two Gentlemen of Verona: Critical Essays* (1996). Broad range of critical essays from Samuel Johnson and William Hazlitt up to 1996 in Part I; Part II has a shorter section with a selection of reviews of productions from 1821 to Thacker's 1991 RSC production.

Shapiro, Michael, *Gender in Play on the Shakespearean Stage: Boy Heroines and Female Pages* (1994). Useful introduction to theatrical cross-dressing; chapter 4, "Bringing the Page Onstage: *The Two Gentlemen of Verona*," focuses on the role of Julia, pp. 65–91.

Williamson, Sandra L., and James E. Person, eds., *Shakespearean Criticism*, vol. 12 (1990). Gives an overview of stage history, reviews, and retrospective accounts of selected productions.

AVAILABLE ON DVD

Two Gentlemen of Verona, directed by Don Taylor for the BBC Television Shakespeare Series (1983, DVD 2005). Entertaining version with Tyler Butterworth as Proteus, Joanna Pearce as Silvia, Tessa Peake-Jones as Julia, John Hudson as Valentine, and Paul Daneman as the Duke of Milan.

REFERENCES

1. Marc Norman and Tom Stoppard, *Shakespeare in Love* (1999), p. 18.
2. Benjamin Victor, *The Two Gentlemen of Verona. A Comedy* (1763). Advertisement.
3. Victor, *The Two Gentlemen of Verona.*
4. Charles Beecher Hogan, ed., *The London Stage 1660–1800. Part 5: 1776–1800* (1968), p. 694.
5. *European Magazine*, 1821. Reprinted in June Schlueter, ed., *Two Gentlemen of Verona: Critical Essays* (1996), p. 233.
6. *Saturday Review*, 6 July 1895.
7. *The Times* (London), 30 December 1841.
8. *The Times* (London), 15 December 1848.
9. *The Times*, 15 December 1848.
10. George Bernard Shaw, *Saturday Review*, 6 July 1895, reprinted in Schlueter, *Two Gentlemen of Verona*, pp. 238–9.
11. Shaw, *Saturday Review*, reprinted in Schlueter, *Two Gentlemen of Verona*.
12. Charles H. Shattuck, *Shakespeare on the American Stage: From Booth and Barrett to Sothern and Marlowe* (1987), p. 89.
13. *The Times* (London), 20 April 1938.
14. A. B. Walkley, quoted in Schlueter, *Two Gentlemen of Verona*, pp. 243–4.
15. J. C. Trewin, *Shakespeare on the English Stage 1900–1964: A Survey of Productions.* (1964), pp. 30–1.
16. *The Times* (London), 25 April 1910.
17. *The Times* (London), 16 April 1925.
18. *The Times* (London), 20 April 1938.
19. Muriel St. Clare Byrne, "The Shakespeare Season at The Old Vic, 1956–57 and Stratford-upon-Avon, 1957," *Shakespeare Quarterly* 8 (1957), pp. 469–71.
20. Berners W. Jackson, "Shakespeare at Stratford, Ontario, 1975," *Shakespeare Quarterly* 27 (1976), pp. 25–7.
21. Jackson, "Shakespeare at Stratford, Ontario, 1975."
22. James P. Lusardi, *Shakespeare Bulletin* 2–3(12–1) (1984/85), p. 13.
23. *Guardian*, 21 January 1975.
24. *The Times* (London), 21 February 1975.

25. Jean Peterson, "*The Two Gentlemen of Verona,*" *Shakespeare Bulletin* 9(1) (1991), pp. 33–4.
26. *Evening Standard,* 22 August 1996.
27. *Time Out,* 5 May 2004.
28. *What's On,* 12 May 2004.
29. Bertocci's script was an internet sensation in 2009, though it has so far remained unproduced. www.runleiarun.com/lebowski/.
30. Anne Barton (1974), quoted in 1992 RSC program.
31. A. Alvarez, "Dark-varnished Comedy," *New Statesman* LIX (1517), 9 April 1960, p. 518.
32. Alvarez, "Dark-varnished Comedy."
33. Peter Thomson, *Shakespeare Survey* 24 (1971), p. 120.
34. B. A. Young, *Financial Times,* 24 July 1970.
35. Gareth Lloyd Evans, *Guardian,* 24 July 1970.
36. Roger Warren, "Interpretations of Shakespearian Comedy," *Shakespeare Survey* 35 (1982), pp. 142–3.
37. Rex Gibson, *Times Educational Supplement,* 3 May 1991.
38. Margaret Ingram, *Stratford Herald,* 26 April 1991.
39. Russell Jackson, *Shakespeare Quarterly* 50 (1999), p. 202.
40. Michael Billington, *Guardian,* 22 October 2004.
41. Patricia Tatspaugh, *Shakespeare Quarterly* 56 (Winter 2005), p. 477.
42. *The Times* (London), 6 October 1960.
43. John Russell Brown, *Shakespeare Survey* 41 (1961), p. 132.
44. Peter Roberts, *Plays and Players* 17(12) (September 1970), pp. 28–9.
45. Young, *Financial Times,* 24 July 1970.
46. Eric Shorter, *Daily Telegraph,* 24 July 1970.
47. Young, *Financial Times,* 24 July 1970.
48. Harold Hobson, *Sunday Times* (London), 26 July 1970.
49. Warren, "Interpretations of Shakespearian Comedy," pp. 143–4.
50. Stanley Wells, *Times Literary Supplement* 4094, 18 September 1981, p. 1071.
51. Claire Armitstead, *Financial Times,* 19 April 1991.
52. Benedict Nightingale, *The Times* (London), 19 April 1991.
53. Peter Holland, *English Shakespeares* (1997), pp. 89–90.
54. Robert Smallwood, *Shakespeare Survey* 52 (1999), p. 230.
55. Alastair Macaulay, *Financial Times,* 27 February 1998.
56. Billington, *Guardian,* 22 October 2004.
57. Brown, *Shakespeare Survey* 41, p. 129.
58. W. H. W., *Birmingham Mail,* 6 June 1960.
59. Hobson, *Sunday Times,* 26 July 1970.

60. Roberts, *Plays and Players*, p. 28.
61. *Chronicle & Echo Northampton*, 25 July 1970.
62. John Higgins, *The Times* (London), 26 August 1981.
63. Nightingale, *The Times*, 19 April 1991.
64. Margaret Ingram, *Stratford Herald*, 26 April 1991.
65. Georgina Brown, *Mail on Sunday*, 22 March 1998.
66. Smallwood, *Shakespeare Survey* 52 (1999), p. 230.
67. Kate Kellaway, *Observer*, 24 October 2004.
68. Stanley Wells, RSC theatre program 1992.

ACKNOWLEDGMENTS AND PICTURE CREDITS

Preparation of "*The Two Gentlemen* in Performance" was assisted by a generous grant from the CAPITAL Centre (Creativity and Performance in Teaching and Learning) of the University of Warwick for research in the RSC archive at the Shakespeare Birthplace Trust.

Thanks as always to our indefatigable and eagle-eyed copy editor Tracey Day and to Ray Addicott for overseeing the production process with rigor and calmness.

Picture research by Michelle Morton. Grateful acknowledgment is made to the Shakespeare Birthplace Trust for assistance with picture research (special thanks to Helen Hargest) and reproduction fees.

Images of RSC productions are supplied by the Shakespeare Centre Library and Archive, Stratford-upon-Avon. This library, maintained by the Shakespeare Birthplace Trust, holds the most important collection of Shakespeare material in the UK, including the Royal Shakespeare Company's official archive. It is open to the public free of charge.

For more information see www.shakespeare.org.uk.

1. Ada Rehan as Julia (1896–97). Reproduced by permission of the Shakespeare Birthplace Trust
2. Directed by Ben Iden Payne (1938). Ernest Daniels © Royal Shakespeare Company
3. Directed by Peter Hall (1960). Tom Holte © Shakespeare Birthplace Trust
4. Directed by John Barton (1981). Joe Cocks Studio Collection © Shakespeare Birthplace Trust
5. Directed by Fiona Buffini (2004). Manuel Harlan © Royal Shakespeare Company